scrap simple

USING MINIMAL DESIGN
TO CREATE BEAUTIFUL SCRAPBOOK PAGES

Hillary Heidelberg

Memory Makers Books
Cincinnati, Ohio
www.memorymakersmagazine.com

ABOUT THE AUTHOR

Hillary Heidelberg began scrapbooking five years ago after the birth of her first child. Initially she used (and bought) just about every supply out there. She eventually realized that she prefers a cleaner, simpler look for her own pages. Hillary has been published in *Creating Keepsakes*, *Scrapbooks, etc.*, *Simple Scrapbooks*, *Scrapbook Trends* and *Memory Makers* magazine. She was selected as a Memory Makers Master for 2007 and teaches online scrapbook classes at http://www.nycscraps.com. She lives in New York City with her husband, Michael, and their two boys, Luca and Julian. Since marrying Michael, she has downsized her animal menagerie to one black cat named Sunday.

12 11 10 09 08   5 4 3 2 1

Distributed in Canada by Fraser Direct
100 Armstrong Avenue
Georgetown, ON, Canada L7G 5S4
Tel: (905) 877-4411

Distributed in the U.K. and Europe by David & Charles
Brunel House, Newton Abbot, Devon, TQ12 4PU, England
Tel: (+44) 1626 323200, Fax: (+44) 1626 323319
E-mail: postmaster@davidandcharles.co.uk

Distributed in Australia by Capricorn Link
P.O. Box 704, S. Windsor, NSW 2756 Australia
Tel: (02) 4577-3555

Library of Congress Cataloging-in-Publication Data
Heidelberg, Hillary
  Scrap simple / Hillary Heidelberg. -- 1st ed.
     p. cm.
  Includes bibliographical references and index.
  ISBN 978-1-59963-014-4 (pbk. : alk. paper)
  1. Photograph albums. 2. Photographs--Conservation and restoration. 3. Scrapbooks. I. Title.
TR465.H42 2007
745.593--dc22
                      2007034992

Editor: Amy Glander
Designers: Karla Baker, Jeremy Werling
Art Coordinator: Eileen Aber
Production Coordinator: Matt Wagner
Photographers: Tim Grondin, Al Parrish, Christine Polomsky
Stylist: Nora Martini

F+W PUBLICATIONS, INC.
www.fwbookstore.com

dedication

To my husband, Michael, who put up with me and the endless scraps of paper on the living room floor. I really do love you more than scrapbooking.

acknowledgments

To my family, for bearing with me during the last few months as I worked on this book. I know it's been challenging and I appreciate all your patience.

To Luca. I love you more than the sun and the moon and the stars.

To Julian. You are the sweetest, cutest, most lovable baby in the world—yes, the whole entire world.

To my editors, Christine and Amy, for their patience and dedication throughout this entire process.

To Arika, for being there, for listening to me complain, for critiquing my layouts no matter how sick you were of it and for being my friend when I needed one.

To my SBF girls: Sara, Deanna, Paula, Lori, Celeste and Debbie. It's done! Can you believe it? I can't tell you how much I appreciate your support, your ideas, your knowledge and your feedback throughout the entire process. I really felt like you had my back. Thank you for all your inspiration.

Of course, huge thanks go to my contributors: Severine, Tracey, Nichole, Amanda and Celeste. Without you, this book would have been nothing but a big paperweight (OK, maybe not, but still).

I am a mom. That's my most important job right now. Yes, being a mom is tough (yet utterly rewarding) WORK. It's a full time job so often under-appreciated. Yet, it IS a job. My just turned six year old proclaimed the other day that he was so glad that I didn't work away from home. I, too, am grateful I don't work outside the home, but I'm perhaps more thankful that he didn't seem to recognize that his statement and attitude implied that he views me as someone who DOES in fact work…just not away from home. That's it exactly. In fact, if you ask Noah what he wants to be when he grows up, he always begins with "a daddy," followed by his other occupation of choice (lately "making money," whatever that may mean). What a wonderful thing…to be able to raise my sons to value the job of parent, to see that it should and does come first…that it takes dedication and hard work.

So, what does a mom DO? Being a mom means driving around town, prepping craft projects, reading aloud, playing in the backyard, paying bills, creating layouts, taking pictures, kissing boo-boos, teaching about asteroids, sorting laundry and toys (sometimes simultaneously), and laughing at jokes that aren't really jokes. It means knowing why someone is cranky and what to do to help, being able to translate for others, and caring enough to discipline. A mom is the ultimate jack of all trades…someone who makes her living through living itself and accepts that (in general) there is no possibility of promotion. So, regardless of how many lists I try to make of what things I do in a day, or month, or year, the important thing seems to be that I DO these things. Through my actions, I am modeling to my sons what it means to be a parent. And it really is true…actions speak louder than words.

- November 14, 2006

[…] our formation. I call it […]nse. I have these little […] routines, that the boys […]ck to. It makes life […] preventing arguments […]ping me keep track of […]o, whenever we're out, […]s to my right, Noah is to […]ft and Micah is in the […]le. That's just how it is. […]arly, the boys are always […]ckled into their carseats […]re unbuckled oldest to […]oungest to oldest and […]youngest. Asher gets his teeth brushed first during the day; at Noah's first bedtime. Yes, there actually *were* arguments about these things before I set the rules. They're boys…but they know their directions.

my DECISION

I studied acupuncture for four years.

(summers too).

It defined me. Or at least

a part of me.

Then I had my 2nd baby.

And I began to feel the strain of trying to

juggle it all. So

Michael suggested I stop seeing patients.

I thought and I thought and I thought and I thought.

(I am a Libra, after all.)

Did I mention I am very, very **HAPPY** with the trade off?

L'ART DU BAIN

une grande baignoire

beaucoup de mousse

de l'eau tempérée

des jouets qui giclent

des vagues

walking

about on a

cool fall day

explore

discovering

so many

new and

interesting things.

Katherine

1 year old

(Austin, Texas 2006)

LIFE TODAY IS SO TREMENDOUSLY FULL: you work outside the home; you care for your children; you support your partner. You keep the house clean; you manage the bills; you wipe runny noses and always remember to keep toys in your purse. You rush from one activity to the next, trying your best to multi-task and still keep at least the outward appearance of control.

And when the kids are finally asleep, you sneak away to your scrap space for a little "me" time. After staring at your supplies for a while, you finally pick out a few embellishments for your page. But they're not quite the right size, shape or color. After fussing for a while, your page still doesn't look right. You stare at your supplies some more. Your head spins with possibilities. Maybe another strip of patterned paper would do the trick. You spend 30 minutes browsing through your two-foot paper stack. Suddenly your reverie is interrupted by your husband. "Honey? It's midnight. You coming to bed?" Midnight? How could it be midnight already? You look at the mess around you and realize you've done exactly, um....NO pages. None. Zero. Nada. Now how did that happen?

Sometimes there is such a thing as "too much of good thing" (yes, even when it comes to scrapbook supplies). That may be one reason why layouts with a clean and graphic design are becoming more popular. Not only are they less time-consuming, they also put the focus where many scrapbookers feel it belongs—on the photos and the journaling.

Now I'm not saying you need to do away with your supplies (don't give me a heart attack!). But you can learn to understand which supplies are more "usable" and which ones are better purchased as the occasional treat. This book will show you that beautiful layouts don't necessarily need a lot of "schtuff" on them, and in fact, sometimes less is more.

chapter one
CREATING WITH CARDSTOCK

CREATING SCRAPBOOK LAYOUTS with just some basic supplies such as cardstock, letter stickers and a few simple embellishments can be very liberating. You're not debating which patterned paper, chipboard or rub-ons to mix and match. You're not fussing over whether to use the pink flower or the pink tag in the corner. You're simply focused on the basics, so your unique and special story will shine through.

The basic components of a cardstock-only layout are the same as for more complicated ones—just simplified. The first component is the underlying structure, or "bones," of the layout. This includes photo placement, cardstock placement and effective use of white space. I like to think of this as the bones because the additional elements will "hang" on the layout's frame. And if the bones of the layout are not strong, then no matter how much you fuss with it, something will always feel off. Photo selection is the second important component. Choose strong photos that really tell a story. Color selection is the third component to a strong cardstock-only layout. Choose colors that help reinforce the mood you are trying to convey.

It's important to remember that on a cardstock-only layout the eye is not going to be distracted with embellishments and patterned paper, so the basic components become even more critical to creating a successful layout.

four year old

FASHION SENSE

First off, you absolutely love these socks. You call them your "wedding"
socks since we originally bought them for you to wear to your Aunt
Daniella's wedding. Ever since that day, whenever I ask you to please
go and pick out some socks, these are the ones you choose.
Nevermind that you're wearing sneakers or sandals; you still choose
these. I might even *try* to suggest that you go sockless, or maybe
choose some white socks. "But Mom....." you say to me so seriously.
"These look so beauuuutiful." (Summer 2006)

BATMAN
but of course....

And so the story goes. Your super pirate costume that Aunt Daniella had bought for you was all laid out and ready to go on your bed. And up until that fateful Halloween morn, you *did* have your heart set on dressing as a pirate and had practiced sword-fighting and patch-wearing for at least a week. And of course Mommy had searched (and succesfully found, I might add) your "very special" pirate coins that had mysteriously gone missing. A few hours before we were to go trick-or-treating in Brooklyn Heights, you suddenly changed your mind. You wanted, *needed*, to be Batman. But of course. Despite my pleas ("but you love your pirate costume! You're going to look so *tough!!*"), you would have none of it. "Batman." you insisted. So we dug out your old Batman costume, which I had put away for Julian to wear one day. And you put it on, proudly stomping about as you collected your Halloween treats. But of course. (October 2006)

WIZARDS SUPERHEROES and other career options

SUPPLIES

CARDSTOCK: Bazzill

SNAPS: Making Memories

LETTER STICKERS: American Crafts

CHIPBOARD SQUARE: 7gypsies

FONT: Tan Patty and Wendy Medium, TW Cen MT

ADHESIVE: 3L, We R Memory Keepers

Simple Structure By using just two strips of black cardstock to highlight the black in the photo, this layout came together quickly and easily. When I am stuck on what color to use as my accent color, I look to the photo. The black in this photo was a natural choice, and using black cardstock really made the layout pop.

Simple Story My son has been obsessed with superheroes for over a year. Even though I think there's no way I can forget this phase of his childhood, I just might (and so might he!), so it makes a perfect topic for a layout.

Simple Technique Using a corner round can really soften the edges when using cardstock strips. In addition, it helps draw the viewer's eye towards the center of the layout.

COLOR ME HAPPY

One of my favorite ways to choose cardstock colors when I feel stuck is to visit www.colorschemer.com. Simply choose one main color that you'd like to work with, and the site will select 16 other colors that work well with the one you've chosen. How simple is that?

almost first steps

okay, so I didn't grab my camera when I saw your first steps. I was too stunned at how fast you were moving. But I was sure to have the camera handy the next day when you were walking down the street.

Simple Structure Simple color-blocking allows the story to shine through. Curved journaling adds a bit of visual punch and reinforces the theme of a wobbly beginning walker.

Simple Story A toddler's first steps was a moment I hadn't thought to photograph in my first son's life, so I didn't want to miss it with my second son.

Simple Technique If your layout has become too straight or linear, why not shake it up by adding a curve to your journaling? This is easy to do using any one of a number of software programs available including Photoshop, Illustrator, and even a free program called Serif Draw Plus 4.0.

SUPPLIES

CARDSTOCK: Bazzill

RUB-ON LETTERS: American Crafts

FONT: Arial

ADHESIVE: 3L

SUPPLIES

CARDSTOCK: Bazzill

LETTER STICKERS: KI Memories

CIRCLE STICKER:
Memories Complete

CHIPBOARD NUMBER: BasicGrey

PEN: American Crafts

INK: Tsukineko

Simple Structure One large circle sticker keeps the focus of the layout right in the center, where all the action is.

Simple Story Nichole says, "I like to use many different colors of cardstock on a layout and one way to keep it all cohesive is to use stitching. I also think that doodling, even something as simple as adding a few dots, can add a little extra flair. So I added dots around the edge of the circle."

Simple Technique Tearing paper is a versatile technique that requires no supplies and takes very little time.

Simple Structure This is the simplest of simple layouts: two rows of photos with a balanced composition of title and journaling on either end. I wanted to create a classic layout that would stand the test of time. I find that when I have a bunch of photos with varied backgrounds and different subjects, keeping the layout clean allows the photos to draw the viewer in.

Simple Story Traveling to Europe with two young children was challenging, to say the least. I wanted this layout to showcase a range of photos that reflected our experiences traveling as a young family (both the good and the not-so-good!).

Simple Idea When you have photos from different locations and times, unify them with either a row or grid structure. This design creates coherence and unity between discontinuous photos.

SUPPLIES

CARDSTOCK: Bazzill

SNAPS: Making Memories

FONT: Fundamental Rush, Lauren Script Regular, NevisionCasD

ADHESIVE: 3L, 3M, Xyron

Okay, so NYC can be a daunting place to live. I mean, there's the incessant honking, the crowded subways, and the general hubbub of life in a big city. But I grew up here, and nothing really fazes me anymore. Except for one small thing....the parking signs. What the heck? I mean, I rarely drive a car into the city--too much traffic, way too stressful. And when I do, I tend to splurge (on a parking garage. But when I have to park on the street, it's a joke. You should see me walking up and down the street, one eye on my double-parked car, trying to figure out if it's legal for me to park there. One sign says one thing, and then another sign contradicts it halfway down the block. Now you might think, why stress over it? Well, in NYC, if you're caught in a no-parking zone, they TOW your car. Far away. VERY far away. And it costs mucho buckaroos to get it out. Reason #231 why we don't own a car in the city.......(Summer 2006)

SUPPLIES

CARDSTOCK: Bazzill

SNAPS: Making Memories

FONT: Two Peas Airplane

Simple Structure A simple box structure is one of my favorite designs. Not only does the layout come together quickly, the format can be used again and again without losing any of its appeal.

Simple Story I am utterly confused by the signage in New York City, and I figured it would be a fun topic for a layout. Fifty years from now, won't it be cool to see what street signs looked like "back in the day"?

Simple Idea Is there something you encounter in your day-to-day life that makes you wonder "what's that about"? Or is there a trend from pop culture you just don't "get"? Scrap about it! It will make a wonderful layout for future generations.

Simple Structure This layout's structure is really a spin-off on color blocking. By cropping the photos carefully, they fit nicely into the rule of thirds that governs much of simple color block page construction.

Simple Story My son is simply crazy about climbing the rocks in Central Park. Is this a major event you'd normally take photos of? Maybe not. Is it something Luca might like to know about himself when he's older? Definitely. I really like to scrapbook these everyday moments in my kids' lives so they're not forgotten.

Simple Idea I had these fantastic chipboard embellishments that could easily mimic the rocks my son is climbing. But none of them were quite the right color, so I flipped them over to expose the raw chipboard side and voilà! They turned out quite "rock-like," wouldn't you say? Look at your embellishments carefully, and you'll find they may offer many alterable solutions to fit your needs.

SUPPLIES

CARDSTOCK: Bazzill

CHIPBOARD LETTERS: American Crafts

CHIPBOARD EMBELLISHMENTS: American Crafts

FONT: Times New Roman

ADHESIVE: 3L, 3M

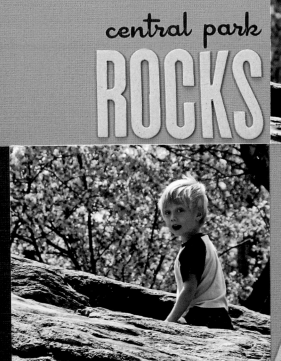

central park
ROCKS

If there's one thing you love to do more than just about anything, it's to go up to Central Park and "rock climb". You clamber on the rocks, inspect the crevices for sticks and bugs and just completely enjoy yourself. It's an activity you and Papa often do together, so I'm pretty sure that's part of the allure. (4.2007)

RULE OF THIRDS

The "Rule of Thirds" is a design principle that divides space within equal thirds. Visualize a grid (or tic tac toe board) of three horizontal lines and three vertical lines. Place the important elements at one or more of the points at which these lines intersect. The result will be a visually appealing layout!

SUPPLIES

CARDSTOCK: Bazzill

FONT: Blue Highway, Carpenter,
Ed Interlock

BRADS: Unknown

Simple Structure This layout personifies simple and clean. Placing everything along one centered column allows the eye to move easily down the elements from title to photo to journaling. Plus, if you forgo the handcut title and replace it with letter stickers or rub-ons, this layout would take about 20 minutes to complete. You gotta love that.

Simple Story My oldest son is very particular about what he wears. But what he thinks looks good and what the entire rest of the world thinks looks good differs just a bit. These were his favorite socks for about five months when he was four years old, and every morning he'd ask me if I remembered to wash them the night before. Ah, the life of a mother.

Simple Idea Line 'em up! Leave plenty of white space and line up your journaling, title and photo. Why? Because it's easy, fun and looks great. What more could you ask for?

A
sweet
lovely
girl.
alli
and
ben's
first
child.

hello.

Welcome
to the
world,
Kylie
Eastman.
We're
glad
you've
joined us.

Simple Structure Say "hi" to the rule of thirds again! Whenever you're stuck, follow this rule: divide your layout into thirds and place an element or grouping in each third.

Simple Story My good friend Alli and her husband had these wonderful shots of their newborn daughter, and I wanted to showcase the photos for a gift. I plan on framing the layout for Alli to hang on her wall, since she is not a scrapbooker.

Simple Technique I often hear scrappers say that journaling upsets the balance of their page design. Try running your text right along the edge of the photos for a simple and clean way to tell your story without compromising your design.

SUPPLIES

CARDSTOCK: Bazzill

LETTER STICKERS: Chatterbox

FONT: Wendy Medium

ADHESIVE: 3L

resistance is
FUTILE

So I'll just assume there was some marketing genius somewhere who decided it would be a great idea to place candy at kids' eye level. Or maybe it was some guy (not a woman!) intent on torturing mothers everywhere. Because every single time we go to the store, Luca eyes the rows upon rows of candy longingly, sometimes even picking up a piece to get a closer look. Then he gives me his plaintive, puppy-eyes look. ......Couldn't have put it up a litttttle bit higher, huh? (February 2007, NYC)

Simple Structure Using columns is a simple way to create a stunning layout. In this example, I used nothing but a column of orange cardstock to offset the rest of the design.

Simple Story I snapped this shot inside our local pharmacy. We went in to buy some toothpaste, but as I returned to the counter, I saw Luca eyeing the candy. He stood there for quite some time before I caught his attention!

Simple Idea When working with photos that have a busy background, I like to use solid cardstock or a muted patterned paper. This prevents the elements from competing with the photo for attention.

SUPPLIES

CARDSTOCK: Bazzill

RUB-ON LETTERS: American Crafts

CHIPBOARD LETTERS: Die Cuts With A View

PHOTO TURN: 7gypsies

FONT: TWCen

ADHESIVE: 3L, Xyron

Simple Structure Three strips of primary colored cardstock form the foundation of this layout. By positioning the text on the upper left amid an expanse of white space, the viewer's eye is drawn to the brief and comical journaling.

Simple Story Every little kid has funny things he or she does, and I'm sure Julian was not the only baby who liked to chew his shoes (please tell me he wasn't alone!). I was trying oh-so-hard to get a cute shot of Julian's face, but he kept putting his foot in his mouth. I finally decided you've gotta work with what you've got!

Simple Technique I cut the title out of some fun patterned paper using a die-cutting tool. The effect of the striped title brings a bit of eye candy to an otherwise straightforward layout. Try doing just one or two "aha!" things on your layout—just enough to make your layout stand out, but not enough to overwhelm the eye.

SUPPLIES

CARDSTOCK: Bazzill

PATTERNED PAPER: American Crafts

PHOTO CORNER: QuicKutz

DIE-CUT TITLE: QuicKutz

FONT: District Thin

ADHESIVE: Duck

A little pepper, perhaps? *gourmand*

SUPPLIES

CARDSTOCK: Bazzill

RUB-ON LETTERS:
Making Memories

LETTER STICKERS:
American Crafts

BRADS: Unknown

FONT: Verdana

ADHESIVE: Herma

Simple Structure Amanda used the complementary colors of blue and orange to create this stunning layout. She clustered a grouping of photos on the left, and then balanced them by placing one large photo on the right. I particularly like how she viewed this two-page layout as one large canvas.

Simple Story Amanda says, "Everyone was just so taken with my sweet baby's full head of hair that I knew I was going to have to do a layout about it. I kept teasing my husband by threatening to go find a beaded jumpsuit and little guitar, and dress our baby up as Elvis. Seriously, the kid was born with sideburns! You gotta document stuff like that!"

Simple Technique Notice how Amanda rounded just one corner of four of her main elements. This ties everything together nicely.

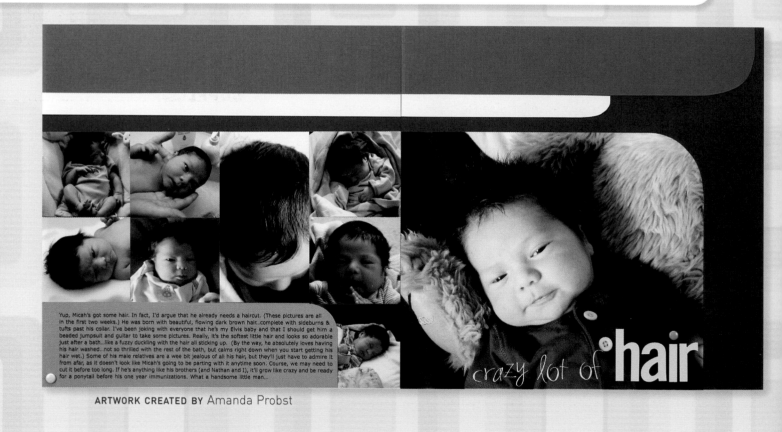

Yup, Micah's got some hair. In fact, I'd argue that he already needs a haircut. (These pictures are all in the first two weeks.) He was born with beautiful, flowing dark brown hair...complete with sideburns & tufts past his collar. I've been joking with everyone that he's my Elvis baby and that I should get him a beaded jumpsuit and guitar to take some pictures. Really, it's the softest little hair and looks so adorable just after a bath...like a fuzzy duckling with the hair all sticking up. (By the way, he absolutely loves having his hair washed...not so thrilled with the rest of the bath, but calms right down when you start getting his hair wet.) Some of his male relatives are a wee bit jealous of all his hair, but they'll just have to admire it from afar, as it doesn't look like Micah's going to be parting with it anytime soon. Course, we may need to cut it before too long. If he's anything like his brothers (and Nathan and I), it'll grow like crazy and be ready for a ponytail before his one year immunizations. What a handsome little man...

crazy lot of **hair**

ARTWORK CREATED BY Amanda Probst

20

Simple Structure The large title that spans the gutter of both pages immediately grabs your attention. Even though this is a two-page layout with multiple photos, Amanda still managed to leave a bit of white space to draw your eye straight to the photos.

Simple Story Amanda says, "This is a simple layout about my eldest surprising me when he read his first book. I wanted to include some of the actual pages for reference. I remember my own mom trying to remember when each of us started reading, so I made a mental note to document the actual start for each of my own sons. I couldn't have been prouder!"

Simple Technique If you want to document the first book your child ever read, why not scan a few pages and include them right on your layout? You can even include "hinges," as Amanda did here, so that the viewer can turn the pages. Trim a slit in your page protector for the pages to fit through. You can hide your journaling below so that it doesn't distract from your layout's clean lines.

SUPPLIES

CARDSTOCK: Bazzill

HINGES: Making Memories

FONT: Century Gothic

ADHESIVE: 3M, Herma

The Little Shop of Physics is a collection of more than 200 hands-on experiments designed for students of all ages. It's put on by Colorado State University as a science outreach program. We caught the tail end of their public open house earlier in the spring...just long enough to know that we definitely wanted to spend more time there. When our homeschool group organized a private field trip for just 25 of us, we were first in line. The timing coincided with Grandma Nancy's visit, so we all had a great time going to each of their four rooms of experiments learning cool stuff. A couple of Little Shop staff stayed with us to answer any questions, but otherwise we were free to simply roam and play as we liked. Each experiment (made, for the most part, with things people can find around the house or at the local hardware store) had a little write up next to it with instructions and the lesson to be learned. In the end, the staffers presented each kid with a special gift...a red plastic strip that magically "says" the phrase "Little Shop of Physics" when you run it between your finger and thumbnail. Cool.

ARTWORK CREATED BY Amanda Probst

Simple Structure Wow! Can you say lots of photos? I simply adore this layout by Amanda. She managed to include a whopping 17 photos on this layout! Yet, it is the use of one large, striking photo in the center that grabs your attention.

Simple Story Amanda says, "We homeschool, so every outing has the potential to be a field trip. However, some are more obvious than others. I try to document those days, not only to prove that we do indeed learn stuff, but to remind the boys of experiences they've had."

Simple Technique Try printing a 6" x 4" (15cm x 10cm) sheet of small thumbnail images to include on your layout. See the sidebar below for instructions.

SUPPLIES

CARDSTOCK: Bazzill

LETTER STICKERS: BasicGrey

FONT: Bookman Old Style

WHITE PEN: Sakura

ADHESIVE: Herma

FOCUS ON PHOTOS

Here's an easy way to place lots of smaller photos on a layout using Photoshop and without wasting any valuable photo paper.

Step One Create a 6" x 4" (15cm x 10cm) file at 300 dpi.

Step Two Open up the first landscape photo that you want to include on your 6" x 4" (15cm x 10cm) collage. Go to Image--→Resize--→Image Size and resize your image to 2" x 1" (5cm x 2.5cm). Set the dpi to 300 and click the Resample Image option. Because you are downsizing the photo, clicking the Resample Image option won't reduce your image quality significantly. If you are including portrait photos, follow this step but simply resize your image to 1" x 2" (5cm x 2.5cm).

Step Three Drag your resized image onto the new file you created in Step One. Position it so it's located in the upper left corner (you can reorder your photos later).

Step Four Continue to open, resize and drag the photos onto your canvas. You should be able to fit a total of 12 mini photos onto a 6" x 4" (15cm x 10cm) sheet of photo paper. When you are done, you can rearrange your photos as you like. Then go to Layer--→Flatten Image.

Step Five Print your mini collage onto a 6" x 4" (15cm x 10cm) sheet of photo paper. You can either crop the photos or simply include the entire block on your layout as is.

Simple Structure The title hugging the edge of the photograph contributes a sense of cohesiveness to an otherwise playful and "open" layout. The seemingly random placement of the circles are actually not so random: Severine has created a careful triangular balance between the title, the upper circles and the lower right circles.

Simple Story Severine says, "Loan cracks me up when he mixes up his colors. I wanted to create a fun and bright design, and the circles were a great way to reflect the overall mood of the layout."

Simple Technique Even when creating a simple layout, there's always room for a little intentional imperfection. When using shapes like circles or squares on your layout, trim the shapes slightly irregularly to lend a homemade feel.

SUPPLIES

CARDSTOCK: Bazzill

CHIPBOARD LETTERS: Heidi Swapp

FONT: AvantGarde Bk BT

HésitAnt

Tu as appris à reconnaître les couleurs

relativement tard et aujourd'hui, tu es hésitant

avec le jaune et le bleu.

Alors tu as trouvé une parade imparable :

Tu réponds toujours : "c'est jaune OU bleu !"

Journaling translation: You learned how to recognize colors relatively late and today you are hesitant with yellow and blue. So you found a great way to answer. You always reply, "It's yellow OR blue."

ARTWORK CREATED BY Severine Di Giacomo

SUPPLIES

CARDSTOCK: Bazzill

CHIPBOARD LETTERS: Heidi Swapp

MINI BRADS: American Crafts

BUTTONS: American Crafts

FELT FLOWERS: American Crafts

RIBBON: American Crafts

FONT: TwCen MT

ADHESIVE: 3M

Simple Structure Severine created a lovely color-blocked layout with a clean border of white space. The soft colors are a perfect choice for a layout about a child's favorite stuffed animal.

Simple Story Severine says, "It was important for me to document this story because it was such a big deal for my little one. I wanted the focus to be on the journaling because in this case it's the story that's really important."

Simple Idea Try pulling out your pile of cardstock scraps and choosing colors that work well together. That way you can create a beautiful layout and use up some scraps at the same time (which is always a good thing!).

Journaling translation: You adopted "Mouton-Mouton" the same evening you decided you would not sleep with your Blankie anymore. It's a mystery why you chose this cuddly toy rather than another, but, anyway, it is always in your arms when you go to sleep. Each evening it is the same ritual: you go to bed, Popi on one side and Mouton-Mouton on the other, and you await the kisses of Dad and Mom to finally be able to sleep and have beautiful dreams as sweet as your cuddly toy.

ARTWORK CREATED BY Severine Di Giacomo

TRUE LOVE. ALWAYS
TOGETHER. SO LUCKY
TO HAVE HIM.
I LOVE YOU SWEETHEART
TOGETHER FOREVER.

ARTWORK CREATED BY Nichole Pereira

Simple Structure Talk about simply stunning! All this layout needs is one fantastic photo topped by a bold, graphic sentiment.

Simple Story Nicole says, "I love to play around with text. For this layout, I used word processing software to create a text box. Within that text box I put a mix of fonts and sizes. It was so simple and quick to create, yet it remains one of my favorite layouts!"

Simple Technique Use photo corners on opposing corners to pull your layout together and lend an even greater sense of cohesiveness to a tight design.

SUPPLIES

CARDSTOCK: Bazzill

RHINESTONES: Heidi Swapp

FONT: Arial

grit.

You and Papa have one thing most certainly in common: your dedication and commitment once you put your mind to something. Like your father you rarely give up once you've decided you need to master something. Also like your father (and definitely unlike me) you don't get frustrated easily. You want to explore your limits, your abilities, and you don't like it when I interfere. I am trying hard to let you learn your own capabilities. And generally, I am pretty laid back when you attempt to scale high walls, or jump off the jungle gym. But I am secretly just a little but happy when you ask me to hold your hand, or step back off that high jump and go round the "safe' way. It's not because I don't want you to grow up. I do. Really. Just not today. (written 4/4/06)

Simple Structure Using bold colors on a white background really makes this photo pop. Adding a simple finishing touch of cardstock borders really keeps this layout fresh.

Simple Story My son is so, well...tough! He just tackles any obstacle and sticks with it until he figures it out. And sometimes his newfound independence leaves me feeling a bit nostalgic for those days when he needed my help doing everything.

Simple Idea Use one large dramatic photo to convey your layout's intention with just a glance.

SUPPLIES

CARDSTOCK: Bazzill

DIE-CUT LETTERS: QuickKutz

RUB-ON STARS: Heidi Swapp

FONT: TW Cen MT

Simple Structure I just loved this gorgeous and funny shot of Michele's daughter. Combined with a clean column of circles, it really pops against the white cardstock background.

Simple Story Michele gave me a few gorgeous photos of her daughter to scrap, but rather than scrap all of them, I simply selected one that conveyed a real sense of her daughter's personality.

Simple Technique Use small brads at the beginning of each line of text to add color and flair.

SUPPLIES

CARDSTOCK: Bazzill

BRADS: Queen & Co.

FONT: Rockwell

- walk in the rain
- smell flowers
- stop along the way
- build sandcastles
- go on field trips
- find out how things work
- tell stories
- say the magic words
- trust the universe.

-Bruce Williamson

Harper 4 months old

THINKING ABOUT MOOD

One of the most important considerations when creating a cardstock-only layout is the mood your layout conveys. Gray-blue tones are wonderful for thoughtful "all-about-me" pages; primary or bright colors are great for kid pages; and earth tones work perfectly with many older photos. There are no hard and fast rules. Of course, I used orange cardstock to create a page about my children making snow angels, and I love it!

PHOTO TAKEN BY Michele Skinner

chapter two

INCORPORATING PATTERNED PAPER

IT'S DEFINITELY EASY to get seduced by all the lovely patterned papers out there. It seems as though every time I turn around there is a new patterned paper just begging to be purchased. But before I do so, I've learned to stop and consider whether I will actually use it. Because there's one thing I know for sure: having lots of product around gathering dust because I simply don't know how to use it, or even want to use it, is a surefire way to stifle my creativity.

It's easy to choose papers that are pretty to look at. But that's not really what you, as a scrapbooker, need in the end. What you need are papers that you can use effectively on your layouts. Are the colors so unusual or garish that you would be hard-pressed to use them with your photos? Is the pattern on the paper so large that it could only be used on a one-photo layout (where the paper would probably take center stage)? So think before you purchase. And if you already have stacks and stacks of patterned paper in your scrap room that deep down you know you will never use, give it to your local school or community center. Then you can get down to creating and make some other people really happy!

making art

During the summer, the neighbourhood parks organization in Battery Park sponsors a bunch of different kid-friendly events. One cool thing they offer is a weekly outdoor art playtime for little kids on Thursdays. Although we only managed to make it for the tail half-hour, Julian had a fantastic time doodling and drawing pictures of what he loudly pronounces to be "papa!!". (May 2007)

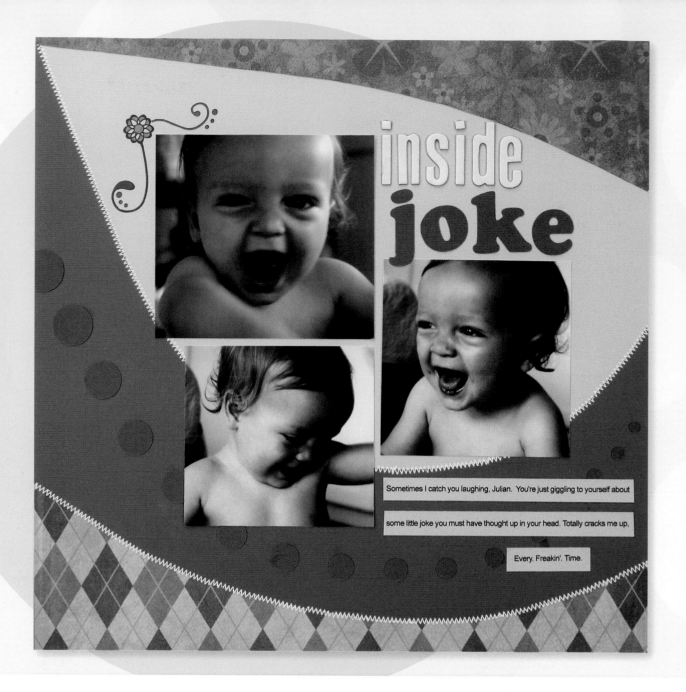

Sometimes I catch you laughing, Julian. You're just giggling to yourself about

some little joke you must have thought up in your head. Totally cracks me up,

Every. Freakin'. Time.

Simple Structure I decided rather than using a blocky pattern, I would cut my paper in swoops to emphasize the playful, fun feeling of the photos. I clustered the photos right at the center of the layout.

Simple Story Julian had this funny habit of breaking into laughter for no reason at all. I managed to grab my camera and snap some shots of him giggling.

Simple Technique Flip your paper over and pencil in some swoops along the expanse of your paper. Use a pair of sharp scissors to trim the curve and adhere it to your paper. It's an easy way to create a unique look.

SUPPLIES

CARDSTOCK: Bazzill

PATTERNED PAPER: Imaginisce

RUB-ONS: Autumn Leaves

FONT: Cooper Black, Traditionell Sans

ADHESIVE: 3L

Simple Structure I don't often use oversized photos on my layouts, but sometimes it just feels right. In this instance, I had one beautiful, evocative photo that perfectly captured the mood I wanted to convey. I placed the photo in between two pieces of subtle patterned paper for a graceful touch.

Simple Story I made a decision to stop working outside of the home for a period of time so I could spend more time with my children and feel less stressed. It was a hard decision since I had worked hard to become an acupuncturist, but a year later I am still very happy.

Simple Technique Use a hole punch to create tiny holes along the length of journaling lines. Then back them with pieces of scrap patterned paper so the color pops from underneath.

SUPPLIES

CARDSTOCK: Bazzill

PATTERNED PAPER: We R Memory Keepers

RUB-ONS: BasicGrey

FONTS: Bebas, Altemus Arabesque, Ballpark Weiner, Futura Mdn

ADHESIVE: Duck, Xyron

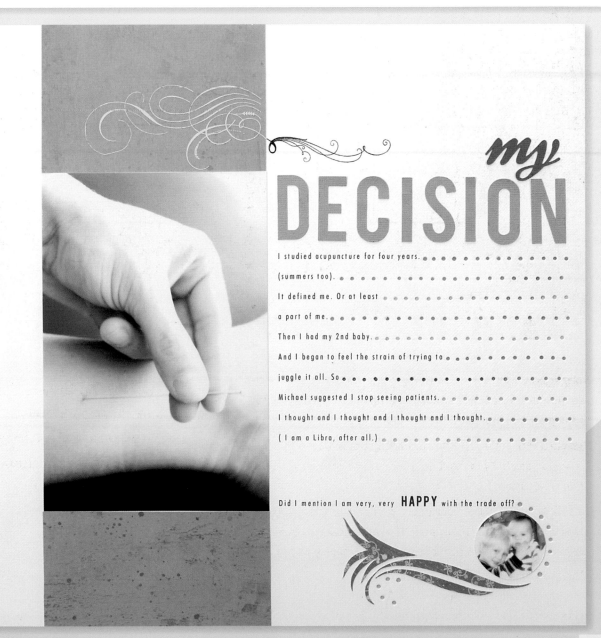

my **DECISION**

I studied acupuncture for four years.
(summers too).
It defined me. Or at least
a part of me.
Then I had my 2nd baby.
And I began to feel the strain of trying to
juggle it all. So
Michael suggested I stop seeing patients.
I thought and I thought and I thought and I thought.
(I am a Libra, after all.)

Did I mention I am very, very **HAPPY** with the trade off?

SUPPLIES

CARDSTOCK: Bazzill

PATTERNED PAPER: Crate Paper

RUB-ONS: Die Cuts With A View

FONT: Ballpark Weiner, Traditionell Sans

ADHESIVE: Duck, Xyron

Simple Structure By intertwining coordinating pieces of patterned paper, this layout evokes the sense of a "path of friendship" throughout life.

Simple Story My son has made some wonderful friendships in his short life and his heart is so open. I used this photo as a way to send a message to my future grown-up son about the importance of maintaining friendships.

Simple Idea Is there a special message you want to send to your future grown-up child? You could just write a letter, but how much more special would a scrapbook layout be?

friends matter

I have a little secret to share with you, Luca. It may not seem like such a big deal, but it's the truth: friends matter. Take your Uncle Whitten: one of the things I've always admired about your uncle is his wonderful ability to maintain long-lasting friendships. You would do well to follow his lead. After family, there's probably nothing more important than having friends you can rely on in hard times, and celebrate with in good times. When I was younger, I spent most of my time either studying or practicing squash. And that was cool, and it served me well in many ways. But it wasn't until I got older that I realized how much I had missed out on by not reaching out and trying to make friends. I learned that the process of making friends, the act of reaching out and providing others with a shoulder to lean on, is not an *optional* part of a happy life. It's the key.

Simple Structure Creating a simple layout doesn't have to mean creating a linear layout. This page uses only one sheet of patterned paper trimmed into a curve. By selecting a different font and color for "Love" in the title, the most important word is emphasized.

Simple Story My children are the most important people in my life. When Julian came along, I wanted to convey to him just how very important he is and how so many people love and support him.

Simple Technique I really loved some of the other papers in this coordinating line, but the patterns were just too big and bold for me to use effectively. So I cut out elements from the paper (e.g., the flower in the upper right) and adhered them to my layout. Try this simple technique the next time you find paper you love with patterns you can't quite figure out how to incorporate into your layout.

SUPPLIES

CARDSTOCK: Bazzill

PATTERNED PAPER: BasicGrey

RUB-ON LETTERS: American Crafts

RUB-ONS: Autumn Leaves

BRADS: Creative Xpress

PEN: Zig

FONT: Impact

ADHESIVE: Duck, Zig

SUPPLIES

CARDSTOCK: Bazzill

PATTERNED PAPER: We R Memory Keepers

SNAPS: We R Memory Keepers

LETTER STICKERS: Arctic Frog

FONT: MK Abel

ADHESIVE: Duck, Xyron

Simple Structure There are so many ways you can take a simple structure like color-blocking and personalize it to suit your photos. The curve in the paper emphasizes the curve of my sister's body as she demonstrates her yoga poses, and the black background makes the warm sheen of these papers pop off the page.

Simple Story My sister has been practicing and teaching yoga for over ten years. She has a talent and affinity for yoga that I wanted to honor in a layout.

Simple Technique To obtain the curve in the patterned papers, I temporarily adhered the paper to a 12" x 12" (30cm x 30cm) glass mat. The glass mat had measurements on it, so I was able to place the patterned paper in exactly the same formation it would end up on the layout. I then used a large circle cutter to cut the semicircle, gently removed the patterned papers from the glass mat and adhered them to my layout.

Simple Structure Select colors that work with your layout and overall theme. In this example, I simply drew colors from the photo. Thankfully, the colors I chose also matched the mood I wanted to convey. The patterned paper on this layout is super subtle, with just a bit of texture adding visual interest.

Simple Story My son and I were butting heads a lot in the months leading up to his fourth birthday. I think we have such similar personalities (strong-willed, stubborn and outspoken) that sometimes it leads to clashes. I wanted to express to him that, no matter what, I will always love him.

Simple Idea Don't be afraid to scrap the difficult aspects of your life or your relationships with your children. When they grow up and have children of their own, think of how much comfort it will give them to know they are not alone in having these same challenges.

SUPPLIES

CARDSTOCK: Bazzill

PATTERNED PAPER: Chatterbox

RUB-ON LETTERS: Making Memories

NUMBER STICKER: American Crafts

FONT: Traditionell Sans

ADHESIVE: Creative Memories, Xyron

SHE CAME. SHE SAW. SHE LEFT.

So.......I'm guessing the Elmo sprinkler wasn't as big a hit as Mom had hoped.

SUPPLIES

CARDSTOCK: Bazzill

PATTERNED PAPER: Die Cuts With A View

LETTER STICKERS: Die Cuts With A View

CHIPBOARD EMBELLISHMENTS: Die Cuts With A View

FONT: TWCen

ADHESIVE: 3M, Duck, Xyron

Simple Structure I wanted to scrap these photos in a filmstrip format to match the long title. This format works well if you have a grouping of photos that convey a story over a period of time (think of your son preparing for a hockey game, playing the game and then making the goal).

Simple Story Michele thought her daughter would be thrilled with a toy that combined two of her favorite things: water and Elmo. Unfortunately, Harper's reaction was not what Michele expected!

Simple Technique To highlight a standout color in your photos (in this example, the red Elmo sprinkler), use only one small, similarly colored embellishment. Sometimes a small, subtle touch can be more effective in drawing the viewer's attention than something more obvious.

Simple Structure You can do a fast and easy layout using patterned paper as your background, and it really adds a nice sense of dimensionality.

Simple Story I was rummaging through some old photos I'd acquired from my mother's house, and I came across this one with a jolt of recognition. I'd really wanted to try to scrap more about myself, so this was a nice addition to my "book of me."

Simple Technique When creating a journaling box on the computer, leave a bit of a margin on one side for an embellishment.

SUPPLIES

CARDSTOCK: Bazzill

PATTERNED PAPER: Daisy D's

EPOXY STICKER: Stemma

RUB-ONS: American Crafts, Die Cuts With A View

LETTER STICKERS: American Crafts

BRADS: Making Memories

FONT: Traditionell Sans

ADHESIVE: Duck, Xyron

When I was young, my dad's business took us to Japan for a few years. I remember leaving the U.S. was devastating, but I also remember having a wonderful time living in Tokyo. We would take trips around Japan, like this one to the Izu Peninsula. I somehow remember this shot, or maybe it's just the memory of seeing this photo again and again growing up. I do remember a huge sense of adventure living in Japan. The customs were so different, everything was so CLEAN, and the people were very, very polite. I also remember having fish for breakfast (*not* a custom we brought back to the States!) 1973.

PHOTO TAKEN BY Eileen Morris

mama.

Pailin did not, at least initially, strike me as someone who was "destined" to be a mother. She was so happy-go-lucky, so sweet, and she was very, very independent. She would jet off to Hawaii or Thailand on a moment's notice. She didn't like to be 'constrained' in any way by the people in her life. Independent for sure. And then, at a later age than some, she got pregnant with Christopher. And while Pailin definitely has kept her independent personality, she now has some-one *dependent* on her, and she's doing such a wonderful job as his mother,(02-06) NYC.

SUPPLIES

PATTERNED PAPER: Hush Papers by Katie Pertiet (Designer Digitals)

BUTTONS: By Stephanie Burt (Pocket Pearls)

STITCHES: Spools of Stitching by Tia Bennet (Two Peas in a Bucket)

FONT: Symphony, Rockwell

Simple Structure The soft background paper works well with the "new mother" theme I was trying to achieve (plus, it conveniently matches my subject's shirt!).

Simple Story I don't get to see my friend Pailin very often, so when I uploaded this photo to my computer after a recent visit, I knew right away I wanted to scrap it.

Simple Technique Don't be afraid to place the focus of your page off-center, as I've done here. Leaving an expanse of pretty pat-terned paper can only serve to highlight your journaling and photo.

Simple Structure Slanting photos adds liveliness and interest to a layout, especially when the photos are not the best.

Simple Story Luca's teachers during his very first year in nursery school were so pivotal in his life, and in our lives as a family. After he's all grown up, I want him to be able to see who these important people were.

Simple Idea When mixing patterned papers, select those with a similar tone or vibrancy. What does this mean? Tone in the technical sense refers to whether a color is light or dim, bright or dull. Vibrant tones tend to pop off the page, whereas duller tones are more muted and less vibrant overall. I wanted to convey a sense of playfulness on this layout so I used patterned papers with tones of a similar vibrancy to keep the feel exciting and fun.

SUPPLIES

CARDSTOCK: Bazzill

PATTERNED PAPER: Luxe Designs, Scenic Route

RUB-ONS: 7gypsies, Die Cuts With A View

LETTER STICKERS: American Crafts

CHIPBOARD EMBELLISHMENT: Fancy Pants

BRADS: Bazzill

FONT: Arial

ADHESIVE: 3L, 3M, Xyron, Zig

SUPPLIES

CARDSTOCK: Bazzill

PATTERNED PAPER: Stemma

LETTER STICKERS: American Crafts

FONT: Tuffy

ADHESIVE: Duck, Xyron

Simple Structure Why make your design more complicated than it needs to be? A simple column of text bounded on the top and bottom by two strips of patterned paper will do the trick!

Simple Story To me, a child's brief passing obsession with a particular toy (or set of toys, as the case may be) is the perfect subject for a scrapbook layout. To be honest, my son's fascination with these toys faded just about a week after I finished this layout, so I'm glad I captured this moment while I had the chance.

Simple Technique Select a font or die-cut alphabet for your title that works not only with your photos, but with your patterned paper as well. The curvy title stickers that I chose complement the circles in the patterned paper, and together highlight the playfulness of the layout's theme.

out of place

On a recent venture to the toy store, Julian, I decided to let you pick out your own toy. Most of the toys you play with are hand-me-downs from Luca, and I figured it would be nice if you had a few more that you could call your very own. You picked out a little 'purse' of bath animals and insisted on carrying it out of the store and around the World Financial Center as I ran some errands. Since I bought you these little guys, they have been everywhere *except* the tub. You take them to bed, you play with them in your room, and you take them to the park. I captured this particular shot at our favorite playground (our nickname for it is the 'baby park' since it was designed for toddlers...I am quite sure it has a more official name, but it escapes me). You had lined them up neatly on the bench, right before sharing them with a cute little girl who came over to play. (April 26, 2007 New York City)

peanut butter pLEaSe!

Luca, every day, I ask you the same question: "What would you like for lunch?" and every day you give me the same answer. And now, Julian has the exact same obsession! (Jan 2007)

Simple Structure Use a square to house your photos, and place your title above and journaling below.

Simple Story Every single day my eldest son eats the same thing for lunch. You'd think he would get bored, but no, he loves that peanut butter and jelly sandwich. And now he's got my youngest son on a peanut butter kick!

Simple Technique Print your photos in a group on a sheet of 8.5" x 11" (22cm x 28cm) photo paper. That way you can save time determining how to arrange your photos, since they're already printed out and ready to use.

SUPPLIES

CARDSTOCK: Bazzill

PATTERNED PAPER: Scenic Route

RUB-ONS; Die Cuts With A View

CHIPBOARD LETTERS: Heidi Swapp

FONT: Goudita Sans Heavy, Share Regular

ADHESIVE: 3L, Xyron

making art

During the summer, the neighbourhood parks organization in Battery Park sponsors a bunch of different kid-friendly events. One cool thing they offer is a weekly outdoor art playtime for little kids on Thursdays. Although we only managed to make it for the tail half-hour, Julian had a fantastic time doodling and drawing pictures of what he loudly pronounces to be "papa!!". (May 2007)

SUPPLIES

CARDSTOCK: Bazzill

PATTERNED PAPER: Imaginisce

BUTTONS: MOD

BRADS: Making Memories

STAR: Imaginisce

RUB-ON LETTERS: American Crafts

FONT: Rockwell

ADHESIVE: Duck, Xyron

Simple Structure It's possible to create a fun layout using only a few patterned paper scraps and it's easy, too. The secret? Use paper from the same manufacturer! Why waste all that hard work they put into color coordinating the papers for you?

Simple Story There are only a few activities Julian and I get to do "just the two of us," and this is one of them. His concentration while painting was definitely a moment I wanted to capture.

Simple Technique To give your layout even more "pop," use white cardstock as your background paper. And when you're stuck for what to do with all those fun little embellishments you've acquired, try clustering them in a group for a clean, vibrant effect.

Simple Structure Tracey saved herself the time and effort of sorting through her (undoubtedly large) patterned paper collection by selecting coordinating papers from the same line.

Simple Story Tracey says, "My husband came home from work and told me about this statistic he heard on the radio that morning. That evening, when our son was asking his bazillion questions in the van, I decided to test my husband's theory. Pen and paper in hand, I wrote down every question while riding in the dark. It doesn't surprise me our son surpassed the estimate."

Simple Technique Create a curve in your layout by trimming your different patterned papers with a large circle cutter, and then piecing them together like a jigsaw puzzle.

SUPPLIES

PATTERNED PAPER: BasicGrey

LETTER STICKERS: BasicGrey

TAG: BasicGrey

FONT: Cafe Rojo (tag, question mark), Avant Garde

ADHESIVE: Tombow, We R Memory Keepers

6:55 pm
What does orange mean? Why can't we drive there? Why is there bumps? Dad, when Emily is asleep, can I make a track on the floor? Can I have juice when we get home? What's my nickname? Is there purple on the map? What time are we going to be home? What time are we going to be home? (again) Can I come with you to let Lela's dogs out? Mom, what time are we going to be there? Did I already said 9? Can I open my window? Well can you put on some air from me cuz I need air? Can I close it cuz I changed my mind? What time are we going to get home? Now how many? Still just 6? That is where our house is gonna be?
7:20 pm

Summary: 19 questions in 25 minutes, driving home from Virginia Beach

???
THE average
5-YEAR-OLD
asKS 437 QUESTiONS
PER Day
IF YOU DO THE CALCULATiON
my 5-YEAR-OLD
asKS 741
???

5 16

ARTWORK CREATED BY Tracey Odachowski

SUPPLIES

CARDSTOCK: Bazzill

PATTERNED PAPER: Hambly

RUB-ON LETTERS: American Crafts

CONCHOS: Scrapworks

FONT: Abadi MT condensed

ADHESIVE: Tombow, We R Memory Keepers

Simple Structure This layout is the perfect example of how to effectively use a paper with a bold pattern. The two stalks on the flowers complement the theme, and because the design is quite simple and clean, the focus remains on the journaling and the photo.

Simple Story Tracey says, "I couldn't help but scrap this priceless photo, and I really wanted my journaling to reflect everything going on behind the scenes."

Simple Technique Dividing your layout into three sections—patterned paper, photos and journaling—is a great way to scrap just about any precious memory. The layout will remain as timeless as the photo.

I cannot even begin to describe what a typical picture of the two of you this is. Gabe, the king of drama, making faces, looking bored, or generally doing pretty much anything to get a laugh out of anyone. Then there is Emily, the tongue queen. I think her tongue stays out of her mouth more than it stays in, which is why she has the nasty rash on her chin that I can never get rid of. Of course, the faces might have been a direct result of what waited for them on the bench with Daddy. Doritos. The bribe to get them to let me take pictures. Gabe probably wanted to get back to them. Emily probably wanted to lick what little crumbs may remain on her lips. So I get these faces. The funny little faces I see every day. The faces that constantly crack me up, amaze me, and torture me. It's really what having my camera in front of you is about, anyway - catching the every day. I love you guys!

September 17, 2006

the two of You ☐ ☐ ☐ ☐ ☐

ARTWORK CREATED BY Tracey Odachowski

44

Simple Structure Using shapes to emphasize your theme is a great way to add visual impact and emotional meaning to your layout.

Simple Story Nichole says, "I love circles! They create movement and design interest, and they are super easy to create. The easiest way is to use a circle cutter, so you don't have to worry about measuring or cutting perfectly. This made it so much easier to create the concentric circles on this layout."

Simple Technique Incorporating circles on your layout is easy to do with all the fabulous circle cutters on the market today. When creating your design, try overlapping circles, trimming in different sizes and using multiple patterns of paper.

SUPPLIES

CARDSTOCK: Bazzill

PATTERNED PAPER: Scenic Route

CHIPBOARD LETTERS: Heidi Swapp

BRADS: American Crafts, Junkitz

45

Simple Structure Enlarging one photo that really speaks to the mood of your page is an effective building block for a great composition.

Simple Story Amanda says, "I just love these pictures of my sweet Micah by the river. I did another version of this layout with color photos for my in-laws. But I found I prefer the black-and-white photos because they focus your attention on Micah's expressions and allow me more freedom in selecting coordinating papers."

Simple Technique Use a light color for the background paper to allow your patterned paper and photos to pop. Also, be aware of how you cut your patterned paper. In this layout, the angled lines of the striped paper really complement the photo below them and move your eye from left to right.

SUPPLIES

CARDSTOCK: Bazzill, Prism

PATTERNED PAPER: Scenic Route

RUB-ON LETTERS: American Crafts

PEN: Sakura

ADHESIVE: 3M, Herma

Simple Structure What a wonderful use of this simple, repeating patterned paper! And framing that one perfect photo with a series of journaling strips really adds a beautiful touch.

Simple Story Celeste says, "I have an affinity for photographing my kids' hands with objects in them—snails, bugs, frogs, apples. I love how this fresh-picked apple looks in my son's small hand. The circle keeps your eye on the photo and invites you to read the journaling.

Simple Technique Sometimes creating a layout of an object (or in this case, a hand holding an object) can convey so much that individual faces aren't even necessary.

SUPPLIES

CARDSTOCK: Stampin' Up

PATTERNED PAPER: Scenic Route

CHIPBOARD LETTERS: Scenic Route

FONT: TW Cen MT

When I was a little girl, every September we would head to the orchard and pick three or four bushels of apples. I remember climbing the trees and eating so many of the crisp, tart apples that my stomach hurt. This is our second year apple picking together. While we usually only come home with a couple dozen apples, you love the experience just the same. Your favorite this year was using the picker to get them off the trees. You probably eat more apples than we take home and you can't resist the cider or the delicious apple pie with whipped cream. I can't wait to go back!

apple

WHAT NOW?

So what do you do with all that bold, hard-to-use patterned paper that you've collected over the years? Some ideas include handcutting the large designs and using them as accents on your layouts, or finding other matching papers that will complement the ones already in your stash. Another option is to just be daring and embrace bold patterns and colors for a fun and funky creation.

ARTWORK CREATED BY Celeste Smith

47

chapter three
ADDING EMBELLISHMENTS

PLAYING AROUND WITH EMBELLISHMENTS might just be my favorite part of scrapbooking. There's something innately pleasurable about sorting through my containers of brads, snaps and doodads to find just the right one for the layout on my scrap table. And sifting through my stack of rub-ons and stickers just makes me plain happy.

Specific-themed embellishments are great when bought in moderation and for a specific project. But I find it much more enjoyable (and productive!) to keep as the bulk of my stash the far more versatile "open-ended" embellishments. These include such items as buttons, stitches, hearts, brads, snaps and flourishes.

What makes these embellishments more versatile? Because they are fairly non-specific, you can use them on a variety of pages, from holiday layouts to soccer layouts. And because they're "basic," they never go out of style. Try working with just a small collection of these basic embellishments on your next few layouts, and see how your style evolves. You just might surprise yourself! The layouts in this chapter will provide you with lots of inspiration.

my bubblegum Extra gum, my big black sunglasses, my Moleskin notebook and faber-castell pen, Rosebud Salve-addicted!!!-

purchased from Ricky's, my new Sidekick-nothing like instant messaging from the park!.and, lest O forget! my house keys.

Essentials.

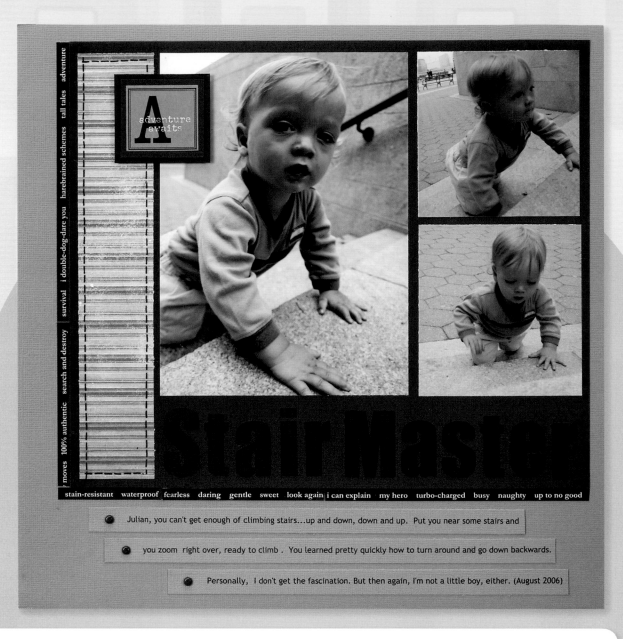

Julian, you can't get enough of climbing stairs...up and down, down and up. Put you near some stairs and

you zoom right over, ready to climb . You learned pretty quickly how to turn around and go down backwards.

Personally, I don't get the fascination. But then again, I'm not a little boy, either. (August 2006)

SUPPLIES

CARDSTOCK: Bazzill

STICKERS: 7gypsies

RUB-ONS: Die Cuts With A View

BRADS: Creative Xpress

FONT: Blue Highway, Impact

ADHESIVE: Duck, We R Memory Keepers

Simple Structure A simple layout with a matted box of photos is easy to create when you have limited time. The sticker embellishment on the upper left was matted on cardstock and then mounted on a pop dot to add a bit of dimension.

Simple Story Here's another layout showcasing one of the many fleeting obsessions of childhood—in this case, my youngest son's love of climbing stairs.

Simple Technique If you want your journaling to carry less visual weight, try cutting your journaling into strips. Add a brad or other small embellishment to "anchor" the strips.

Simple Structure Since it was the story I wanted to highlight here, I used one photo across the top that I altered in image-editing software so the colors gradually move from black-and-white to color. I selected this shot because my son was looking "off" the page, as though into the future.

Simple Story The journaling tells it all in this instance. Happily for us, Julian started talking (a lot!) just a few weeks after I completed this scrapbook page.

Simple Technique Journaling directly onto your photos is not a new technique, but it's definitely one worth revisiting. If possible, select a photo that has plenty of empty space on one side. Alternatively, use image-editing software to blur a photo with a distracting background so that you have a reasonably blank canvas on which to journal.

SUPPLIES

CARDSTOCK: Bazzill

PATTERNED PAPER: We R Memory Keepers

CHIPBOARD FLOURISH: Everlasting Keepsakes

FONT: Creampuff, Wendy Medium

ADHESIVE: 3L, 3M

When you were about 14 months old, I began to notice that you didn't really say much at all. I wasn't really that worried. True, your brother Luca was really verbal by that age, so a part of me was definitely "aware" that you weren't talking very much. But you definitely understood things, and loved to babble and sing songs to yourself (Happy Birthday in particular). At your 18 month checkup in December, the doctor asked the standard litany of questions. Then: "Does he have a good vocabulary? Does he say mama? Papa?" I could only answer no. You had mama down, but for papa, you said "bobby". She recommended early intervention. Nothing to be concerned about, she assured me. But still. So, now you're 19 months, Christmas has passed & still haven't called for the appointment. Why? I don't know. A part of me thinks the doctor is being overly cautious. But maybe I just don't want to think that you might need help from an outsider, from someone other than your mama or your papa. Because that's what we're there for. We're supposed to be take care of you, be able to provide for all your needs. We're supposed to help you learn to talk, learn to walk... I know I'll make the call. I will. Tomorrow.

"bobby?"

ACCENTS THAT STAND THE TEST OF TIME

With so many fun and exciting embellishments out there, it's no wonder that the average scrapbooker's stash is overflowing with accents for every theme imaginable. These are great to have in moderation. But when it comes to the bulk of your stash, embellishments like flourishes, brads, stars and simple circle stickers are staples. By having these "basics" in your arsenal, you'll never have to dig for the perfect embellishment because all of them are well-suited to almost any theme or page topic.

SUPPLIES

CARDSTOCK: Bazzill

PATTERNED PAPER: Fancy Pants

SNAP: We R Memory Keepers

CHIPBOARD FLOURISH: Fancy Pants

CHIPBOARD LETTERS:
Making Memories

PEN: Sakura

ADHESIVE: 3L

Simple Structure Flourishes—whether chipboard, rub-on or hand-drawn—are so versatile. They can be used for a formal wedding layout or for a layout such as this one to add softness and a sense of intimacy.

Simple Story I caught this shot of my husband and our son one morning as I was rushing about getting our eldest ready for school. I always try to keep my camera ready (and the battery charged!) to be sure I don't miss these little moments.

Simple Technique If a store-bought embellishment doesn't quite fit your needs, don't hesitate to do a little simple "altering." On this layout, I wanted to use the chipboard flourish, but I wanted it to "butt up" against the edge of the photo mat. So I simply trimmed part of the embellishment to make it align perfectly.

the ritual.

Just about every morning, Julian, you insist that Papa sit with you by the window. The two of you look down on the street below, pointing out the taxis and buses as they go by. You look at the boats as they move down the Hudson. You get your little smudgy fingerprints all over the window. And Papa patiently sits on the windowsill encouraging your observations. (Summer 2006)

When we visited Gaga in Florida and she presented you with a snazzy dirt bike, you were more than a little thrilled. Now every time you visit Grandma's house you'll have a bike of your own, ready to roll. (January 2007)

Simple Structure The angled photo and other elements add a sense of play to this layout. Use journaling strips instead of a clunky block of text to lessen the visual weight on the bottom of the layout.

Simple Story My son was thrilled when my mother presented this bike to him. I wanted to create a fun layout documenting his joy.

Simple Idea Use long rub-ons as borders for your photos to make them stand out. Because they "hug" the edge of the photos, they can add some visual excitement without drawing the eye away from the centerpiece of the layout.

SUPPLIES

CARDSTOCK: Bazzill

PATTERNED PAPER: Scenic Route

RUB-ONS: BasicGrey, Luxe Designs

CHIPBOARD LETTERS: American Crafts

FONT: Elementary Light SF

ADHESIVE: 3M, Duck, Xyron

SUPPLIES

CARDSTOCK: By Toni Berman (My Digital Muse)

FELT LETTERS: By Katie Pertiet (Designer Digitals)

FELT FLOWER: (Designer Digitals)

STITCHES: Spools of Stitches by Tia Bennet (Two Peas in a Bucket)

FONT: Impact, Lacuna Regular, Pegsanna

TOOLS: Roughed Up Tool Kit by Rhonna Farrer (Two Peas in a Bucket)

Simple Structure On this layout, I wanted to feature a few photos cropped to show the relevant detail. Using a simple box structure is a great way to accomplish this, especially if you don't want to convey a "timeline" effect.

Simple Story My friend Jennifer sent me these sweet photos to scrap, and I was touched by the everyday interaction of a little girl with her favorite toy.

Simple Idea When using embellishments, give some thought to the material they're made of. The felt letters and embellishment used here, while admittedly digital, convey a softness and warmth that is just perfect for a layout about a girl and her cuddly toy.

the Dragon & the PRINCESS

Once upon a time there was a princess name Katie who lived in a modest castle in the fair village of Austin, Texas. One day, Katie was attacked by an evil dragon. But faced with the princess' cute smile and endearing giggle, the dragon soon realized he was no match, and relented. The dragon now lives happily on a shelf in the princess' room, and hasn't breathed (real) fire since.

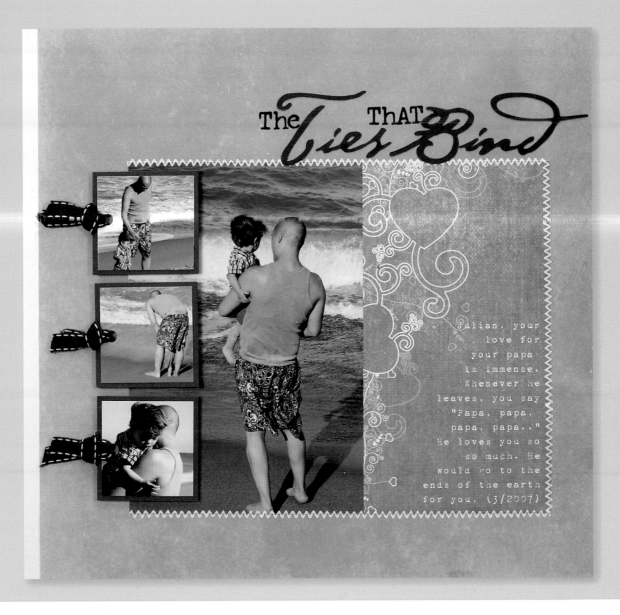

Simple Structure One large, evocative photo edged by smaller shots can create an astonishing layout.

Simple Story While preparing for the birth of our second child, neither my husband nor myself could really believe we would love him or her as much as we love our first. But when Julian was born, our hearts just doubled in size. I created this layout to showcase how much Michael loves Julian and how close they are.

Simple Technique Using tied ribbon as an embellishment can evoke a sense of "closeness" in a layout, and is a wonderful technique to use when showcasing the love between a parent and a child. Another great idea is to try digital brushes, which you can print directly on photo paper or cardstock.

SUPPLIES

CARDSTOCK: Bazzill, We R Memory Keepers

DIGITAL BRUSH: By Jason Gaylor (Designfruit)

RUB-ONS: Die Cuts With A View, Making Memories

RIBBON: Fancy Pants

FONT: Hannibal Lecter, Typewriter New Roman

ADHESIVE: 3L, Xyron

This was such an amazing day. We got married on the beach in Amagansett where I had spent countless days as a child browning myself in the summer sun. We held our reception in an old country house about 15 minutes from the beach. I had reluctantly agreed to a tent, and it was a good thing, 'cause it was much colder than expected. We had a totally vegan dinner, much to the dismay of my mom's meat-loving siblings (sorry, guys). But the crowd was very pleasantly surprised by the vegan wedding cake (looks pretty delicious, right?) We even had real roses trimming the cake. Now, to be totally honest, I don't remember everything about the night--it was such a whirlwind that when it was done, I said I wished I could relive it again, just so I could pay attention to the details. The band, however, I DO remember. Because they ROCKED. They had originally intended to play swing songs, but that wasn't going over too well, so they switched to the wedding stand-by 70's music-and it worked! We all worked up a sweat, dancing and singing at the top of our lungs.. I was so overjoyed to be marrying this fabulous man and I think this picture pretty much sums up how happy I was on that day (and I still am, Michael!) Photo taken Sept 15, 2001.

Simple Structure For this layout, I had only one photo I wanted to feature alongside a longer narrative detailing our wedding day. So to keep it simple, I adhered my photo/journaling block on each side and added rounded corners for a soft touch.

Simple Story I have a huge number of professional wedding photos (which, alas, have yet to go in an album), but this one snapped by my brother really spoke to me.

Simple Technique Remember, three is the magic number. Place three groups of similar embellishments in a visual triangle, as I've done with the rub-on flourishes on this layout.

SUPPLIES

CARDSTOCK: Bazzill

PATTERNED PAPER: American Crafts

RUB-ONS: BasicGrey

CHIPBOARD LETTERS: Making Memories

FONT: MK Abel

ADHESIVE: 3L, Duck, Xyron

Simple Structure By framing the top and bottom of my photo with computer-printed journaling, I allowed for optimal white space while still keeping the layout balanced. I added three simple snaps to add a bit of flourish.

Simple Story We all have our daily must-haves we can't leave home without. Even if I've already left the apartment and made it halfway down the block, I'll head right back if I've forgotten any of them!

Simple Idea Do you have some "must-have" items for your purse? What are they? Gather them together and journal about why you can't leave home without them.

SUPPLIES

CARDSTOCK: Bazzill

PATTERNED PAPER: We R Memory Keepers

SNAPS: We R Memory Keepers

CHIPBOARD LETTERS: Heidi Swapp

FONT: Dear Joe

ADHESIVE: We R Memory Keepers, Xyron

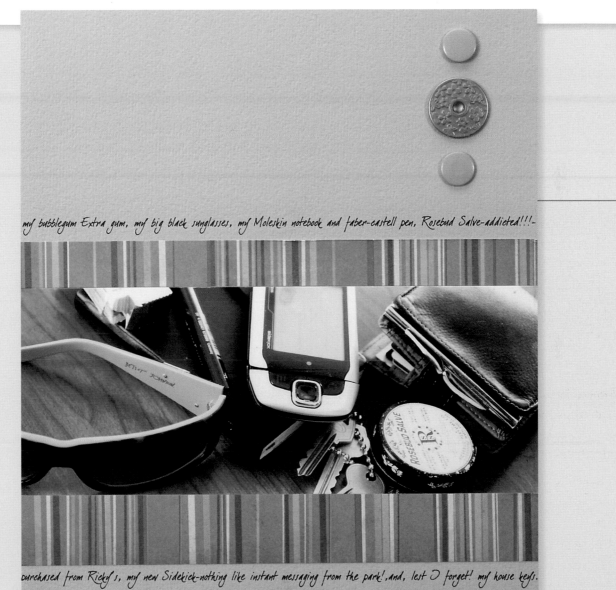

my bubblegum Extra gum, my big black sunglasses, my Moleskin notebook and faber-castell pen, Rosebud Salve-addicted!!!-

purchased from Ricky's, my new Sidekick-nothing like instant messaging from the park!, and, lest I forget! my house keys.

Essentials.

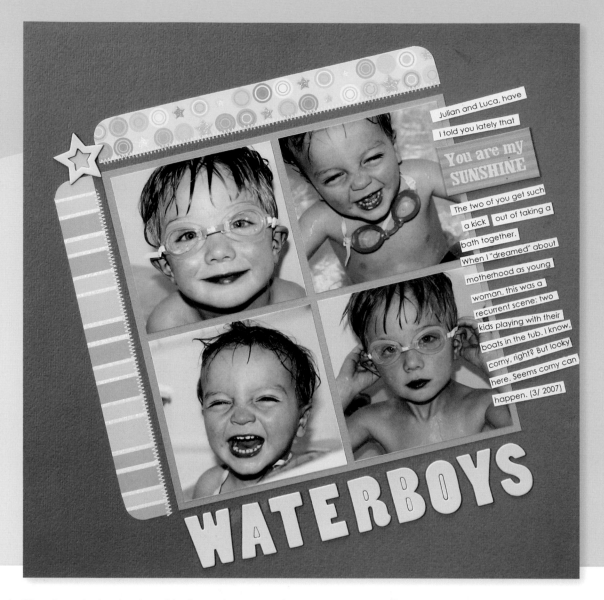

Julian and Luca, have I told you lately that

You are my SUNSHINE

The two of you get such a kick out of taking a bath together. When I "dreamed" about motherhood as young woman, this was a recurrent scene: two kids playing with their boats in the tub. I know, corny, right? But looky here. Seems corny can happen. (3/ 2007)

WATERBOYS

Simple Structure A simple photo block can become a lot more interesting when placed on an angle. To keep the design tight and clean, each side of the block is embellished with either patterned paper, journaling or the title.

Simple Story I've always wanted some shots of my boys in the bathtub together, but the lighting in our bathroom is far from ideal. So when we were visiting my mother, I took these shots in her well-lit bathroom. I am happy with the results and even happier their goggles matched some of my favorite paper!

Simple Idea As easy way to journal is to incorporate "word" or "phrase" embellishments as part of your text, as I've done here.

SUPPLIES

CARDSTOCK: Bazzill

PATTERNED PAPER: Die Cuts With A View

RUB-ONS: Die Cuts With A View

CHIPBOARD LETTERS: Die Cuts With A View

CHIPBOARD STAR: American Crafts

CHIPBOARD PHRASE: Die Cuts With A View

FONT: Tw Cen MT

ADHESIVE: 3L

Simple Structure This layout was really about the story, so I chose just one goofy photo of my son to mix with some bright, playful paper. The column of text hugs the edge of the photo to maintain the sharp look of the layout.

Simple Story My son and I are constantly making up crazy games. He's definitely inherited my offbeat sense of humor, and I wanted to document this part of our relationship.

Simple Technique Think of unusual ways to use basic supplies like brads. It will not only stretch your creativity, it will also put your favorite tried-and-true items to great use.

SUPPLIES

CARDSTOCK: Bazzill

PATTERNED PAPER: Die Cuts With A View

BRADS: Queen & Co.

CHIPBOARD LETTERS: Heidi Swapp

RUB-ON LETTERS: Imagination Project

FONT: Rockwell

ADHESIVE: 3L

What if I were a **broken machine**

I am totally into playing hypothetical word games like "what if...?" and "would you rather...?" Unfortunately, these games don't hold the same allure for Michael. Luckily, I have found a new partner. Luca and I started playing this made-up game we call "What If i Were A Broken Machine" and then you add on something like "and I had eyes on my belly" or " and my mouth was on my hand" (I know, a machine never even comes into it!) Then we each go on to list the ways our lives would be different. Like: "you would have to cut holes in your shirt to see" or "you wouldn't need a fork 'cause you could just stick your hand in the bowl". I definitely think Luca has inherited my sense of humor. And Michael, you're now officially off the hook! (4/07)

BONKERS FOR BRADS

My favorite embellishment just has to be the mini brad. Not only are they inexpensive, they take up very little room and are endlessly versatile. Mini brads can be arranged into shapes, as I did on my "From Me to You" layout on page 110, or they can be used as an easy, fast accent on the edge of a photo/journaling block.

SUPPLIES

CARDSTOCK: Bazzill

BUTTONS: Autumn Leaves

STICKERS: Heidi Grace

CHIPBOARD LETTERS: Scenic Route

FLOWER: Prima

PEN: American Crafts

EMBROIDERY THREAD: DMC

Simple Structure I love these playful photos and how they're arranged in a staggered manner. As this layout shows, simple doesn't have to mean "graphic." It can be executed in a variety of styles.

Simple Story Nichole says, "I never stitched a single thing until I stitched on paper. It truly is the simplest embellishment. It isn't bulky; the colors are endless; it adds that special touch to a layout; and it creates a sophisticated look. For this layout, I wanted to keep the embellishments light because I adore these pictures."

Simple Technique If you own a sewing machine, why not use it on your scrapbook layouts? Sewing is a quick and easy way to add softness. An even easier, if slightly more time-consuming, way is to simply stitch by hand.

ARTWORK CREATED BY Nichole Pereira

60

Simple Structure When creating a layout with a simple structure, use subtle, well-placed embellishments to catch the viewer's eye. Here, Severine used a delicately embellished circle in the center of her photos to capture a sense of movement.

Simple Story Severine says, "I really wanted to document this moment because it was the first time Loan played with this kind of plane. He had so much fun!"

Simple Idea Be sure to ground your embellishments. Place them either on the edge of a piece of patterned paper or on another grounded element. In this example, Severine placed buttons and a metal index tab on the circle to keep these embellishments from floating on the page.

Journaling translation: Fascinated by the flight of two planes at Signal de Bougy.

SUPPLIES

CARDSTOCK: Bazzill

PATTERNED PAPER: KI Memories

CHIPBOARD LETTERS: Heidi Swapp

STICKER: 7gypsies

EPOXY STICKER: Autumn Leaves

BRADS: American Crafts

METAL INDEX TAB: 7gypsies

BUTTONS: SEI

RUB-ONS: Autumn Leaves

FONT: AvantGarde Bk BT

ADHESIVE: 3M

Finally walking.

Becoming independent.

I don't have to carry you everywhere.

You get into even more things than before.

It's just too cute seeing those chubby little legs pounce across the floor.

I've been waiting for the moment that you would walk on your own.

I knew it wouldn't take you to long because you are so eager to do everything that Gabe does.

But, just like your brother, you can't do it when I have a camera handy.

He took his first steps reaching for a Scooby Doo keychain in Kohl's.

WALKING

You took your first steps reaching for a train at Barnes and Noble.

July 20, 2005.

10 1/2 months old.

My camera was at home, charging.

ARTWORK CREATED BY Tracey Odachowski

SUPPLIES

CARDSTOCK: Bazzill

INK: Stampin' Up

DIE-CUT FLOWERS: Urban Lily

ACRYLIC LETTERS: Heidi Swapp

FONT: Abadi MT Condensed

ADHESIVE: Tombow, We R Memory Keepers

Simple Structure Tracey printed her evocative photo and journaling directly onto her cardstock and then added soft title letters.

Simple Story Tracey says, "I was inspired by a shoe ad with a photo emphasizing feet. It seemed like the perfect way to capture some of my daughter's first steps. To this day, I can specifically remember throwing a ball across the room to get her to retrieve it so that I could set up this shot!"

Simple Technique Capture your child's tiny footprint by rubbing an inkpad across the bottom of his or her foot. Just make sure it's not pigment ink, or it will be difficult to wash off!

BROWN'S HARVEST

field trip

This year Daddy accompanied you on your class field trip to Brown's Harvest in Windsor, Connecticut. The morning's activities included a hay ride, choosing a pumpkin, a snack, playing on the hay bales and in the old fire truck. You particularly enjoyed the playground and mini-corn maze they had set up. You came home with a beautiful pumpkin that we carved for Halloween. –October 2005

ARTWORK CREATED BY Celeste Smith

ARTWORK CREATED BY Celeste Smith

Simple Structure To create a well-balanced and eye-pleasing layout without a lot of work, center all your elements in the middle of the page background, as Celeste has done here.

Simple Story Celeste says, "I usually don't produce multi-photo layouts. I really wanted to use the brackets on this layout and none of the photos were spectacular enough to use alone. So I felt a collage of photos would be more appropriate. I created the collage using image-editing software and then printed it as one block."

Simple Technique Cover raw chipboard elements with patterned paper for a fun, easy accent. Simply place your chipboard on the back of your patterned paper and outline the edge with a pencil. Then trim along the pencil lines and adhere the paper to your chipboard.

SUPPLIES

CARDSTOCK: Stampin' Up

PATTERNED PAPER: American Crafts

BRADS: American Crafts

CHIPBOARD LETTERS: Heidi Swapp

CHIPBOARD: Fancy Pants

FONT: Times New Roman

ADHESIVE: 3M, Tombow

SUPPLIES

CARDSTOCK: Bazzill

PATTERNED PAPER: Scenic Route

RUB-ON LETTERS: Autumn Leaves

BRADS: American Crafts

PHOTO TURNS: 7gypsies

JOURNALING STAMP:
Autumn Leaves

STAMPING INK: Unknown

ENAMEL EMBELLISHMENT:
Making Memories

FONT: Tw Cen MT

Simple Structure Severine created a mini collage of photos on a 4" x 6" (10cm x 15cm) canvas, thus allowing for three photos and plenty of white space on her layout.

Simple Story Severine says, "I love to play with embellishments! It's really fun to take some of your favorite things and play with them until each element has found its perfect spot."

Simple Idea Notice how Severine took a number of small embellishments and clustered them on the lower right of her photo collage. When clustering embellishments, keep in mind the importance of proportion when selecting which ones to use. You don't want a photo, accent or other element to be overpowered by a larger element in your design.

Journaling translation: The art of the bath: a big bathtub—a lot of foam—warm water—toys that spatter—waves.

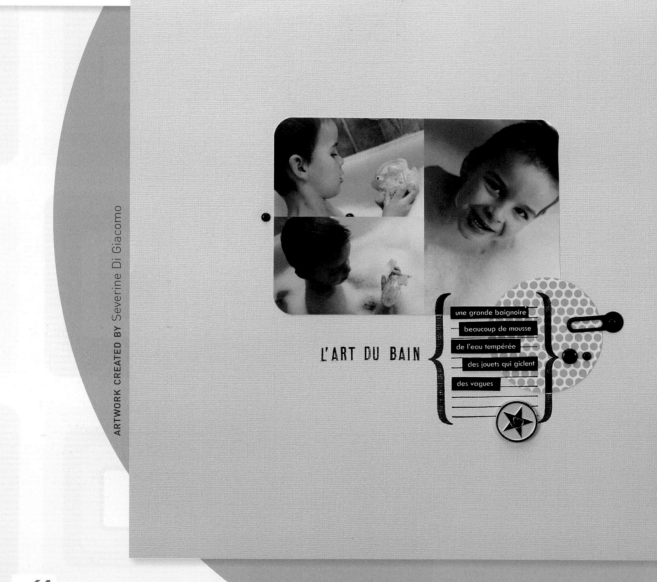

ARTWORK CREATED BY Severine Di Giacomo

let's hear it for the boy

fast

woohoo! i'm so proud of you! you overcame your fear of falling off the bike (with a little help from elbow and knee pads) and learned how to ride without training wheels. go adam! may 2006

LESS IS MORE

If you want to create a simple, clean layout, then moderation is key—especially when adding embellishments. Remember, you want the focus to remain on your photos and journaling. An embellishment-heavy layout not only distracts the viewer, it also takes a whole lot more time to create! In fact, a great rule of thumb when you feel something's "off" on your layout is to remove an item rather than add an item.

Simple Structure Celeste grounded her layout by placing all the critical elements toward the bottom, leaving a wonderful sense of "open sky" above. She clustered her main embellishment below the photo, and then used the orange tape and photo corner to create a visual triangle.

Simple Story Celeste says, "I love white cardstock. Everything pops against a white background, and it lends a clean, sleek look to almost any patterned paper. Both the swoosh and the way I tilted my camera when I snapped the photo add movement to the layout."

Simple Technique When using symmetrical elements like circles or stars, try repeating them in varying sizes, either in the shape of a circle or a simple row.

SUPPLIES

CARDSTOCK: Bazzill

PATTERNED PAPER: Urban Lily

STAR: Heidi Swapp

CHARMS: Queen & Co.

PHOTO CORNER: Heidi Swapp

STICKERS: KI Memories

FONTS: Bluecake, Scrapbook

ADHESIVE: Tombow

chapter four

CREATING TWO-PAGE LAYOUTS

I AM A HUGE FAN OF MULTI-PHOTO, TWO-PAGE LAYOUTS. But I must admit that sometimes the thought of starting (and finishing) one can seem a little daunting. There's so much space to fill and so many different ways of arranging the photos and other elements. But as this chapter shows, you can easily create two-page layouts that are simple, clean and come together quickly.

One trick for putting together a simple, two-page layout is to view both pages as part of one large canvas. This way, when you're placing elements and photos for balance or visual effect, you're taking the entire canvas into consideration.

I often have several photos of events or family gatherings and don't want to choose just one or two to highlight. I want to include three, four or maybe ten photos on my layout. I want to capture and remember all the people, the scenery and the mood, and only a multi-photo, two-page layout will provide enough space. But with so many pieces, I sometimes struggle with maintaining a sharp, clean look. This chapter will showcase some amazing two-page layouts that use multiple photos but still retain a harmonious simplicity.

Celebrating
Spring in Winter

This has definitely been a crazy winter. The weather in January was so ridiculously warm, it felt like spring. I think it got up to something like 68 degrees! Living right on the Hudson River, it's usually WAY too cold in the winter to go out and play, so this day was a welcome respite. We went out to the Cherry Tree Park and you just ran around, enjoying the gorgeous sunny day (which was a good thing, it turns out, since it snowed the next day!!) January 2007

(not-so- scary)

The ^Halloween Tiger

Once upon a time there was a little boy named Julian. His grandma bought him a very very cute yellow and black tiger costume with little fuzzy ears, and Julian wore the outfit for the Halloween party at his brother's school. He looked totally adorable in it. He didn't even try to pull the hat part off, not once. He toddled around in it, to and fro, looking pretty much as cute as a 16 month old can look. But he wasn't scary. Not even a little, tiny bit. (October 2006)

SUPPLIES

CARDSTOCK: Bazzill

PATTERNED PAPER: CherryArte

FONT: Arial, Franklin Demi, Pegsanna

EPOXY STICKER: Autumn Leaves

ADHESIVE: Duck, Xyron

Simple Structure I love the photo on the right, so I enlarged it so that it almost filled the height of the page. The simple black swoosh along the top adds a bit of playfulness as it leads the eye toward the right.

Simple Story My mom bought Julian this outfit, and I thought for sure he would want "out" within a few minutes of my putting it on him. But Julian was quite content to keep the entire outfit on—including the hood—for most of the afternoon.

Simple Idea When trimming a title, either with a craft knife or a die-cutting machine, vary the hue of the letters for a subtle effect.

Simple Structure I managed to fit eight photos on this layout by strategically cropping them to highlight important details. If you don't like to crop out much of the background, be sure to take some long shots of your subject. This way, you can crop the photo to your liking while still retaining some of the background.

Simple Story This was such a fantastic day at the bay in Amagansett, and I wanted to get as many photos as I could on the layout.

Simple Idea Let your patterned paper guide you if you're stuck on which way to go when designing your layout. In this instance, the blue patterned paper reminded me of crashing waves so I trimmed the paper and added my own handcut curves to carry out that theme.

SUPPLIES

CARDSTOCK: Bazzill

PATTERNED PAPER: Scrapworks

CHIPBOARD LETTERS: Heidi Swapp

EYELETS: Making Memories

FONT: Arial

ADHESIVE: Xyron, Duck

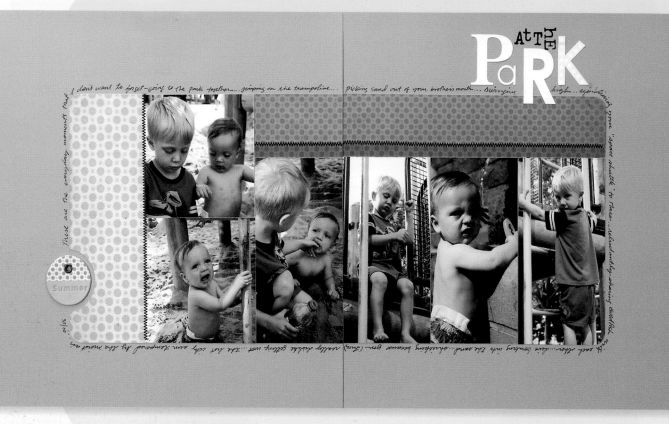

Simple Structure I wanted to create a tight, simple structure of photos interspersed with some subtle patterned paper. That way I could get multiple photos on the layout while still keeping a wide border around the block.

Simple Story A big part of our summer life here in New York City is our daily trips to the wonderful parks in our neighborhood. Luca and Julian love nothing more than to chase each other around the park, play on the slide and splash in the parks' fountains.

Simple Idea Journal around the edge of a photo block in your own handwriting to add a personal touch. Journaling in this way also adds a great border to the entire block.

SUPPLIES

CARDSTOCK: Bazzill

PATTERNED PAPER: We R Memory Keepers

CHIPBOARD TAG: We R Memory Keepers

RUB-ONS: Die Cuts With A View, Making Memories

LETTER STICKERS: Doodlebug

PEN: Sakura

ADHESIVE: We R Memory Keepers

Simple Structure Sometimes an unusual shape is the only embellishment you need to create an eye-pleasing layout.

Simple Story When my son began Tae Kwon Do, at the tender age of four, he was easily distracted in class and often goofed around. But over time he learned that Tae Kwon Do was a place to focus and direct his energies, and I am so proud of him.

Simple Technique To create an oval collage such as this one it's important to arrange your photos so that when you trim the shape, you don't eliminate crucial elements. It takes a bit of practice to get it right, but the effect is worth it. I matted these photos on light blue cardstock, and then used a pen to hand draw the curve, which I then cut out.

SUPPLIES

CARDSTOCK: Bazzill

FONTS: Impact, MK Abel

ADHESIVE: We R Memory Keepers

I am so so proud of you, Luca. You have been so so dedicated to Tae Kwon Do ove rthe last year. Last week, you took your blue belt test and you were amazing. You not only broke a board with your hand (which you had done for your green belt test) but you broke a board with your foot too! On the first try!!! Since you've gotten your blue belt, you love being the one that the teacher calls on to demonstrate the kicks and punches (since, as you like to remind me, you are the "highest ranking" belt in the class. Yes, there have been days when you haven't wanted to go, and that's totally fine. (Heck, we all know there are days I don't want to move either!) But I hope you always remember to have fun, to be a gracious winner (and loser) and to respect your teacher. (February 2007)

CREATIVE PHOTO COLLAGE

A wonderful way to gather lots of photos together is to use a photo collage. You can create the collage in image-editing software and then print it, or you can simply print your photos in a 4" x 6" (10cm x 15cm) size and arrange them on a two-page background. Overlap them so they fill the block size you want to create (be sure to not cover crucial elements of your shots) and trim accordingly.

Simple Structure Sometimes you don't have the most outstanding photos in the world, but you've captured such a special event or moment that you simply must record it on a scrapbook page. That's how I felt about these photos, so I picked the best one to highlight and then cropped the remainder into squares.

Simple Story I am continually amazed by the kindness and patience that Luca gives Julian. Sure, they sometimes quarrel as all siblings do, but it's pretty unusual. When they're older I want them to be able to look at this layout and be reminded of their love for each other.

Simple Idea Work in groups of three. On this layout, I used three tags strategically arranged in a visual triangle to give cohesiveness to the large, two-page spread.

SUPPLIES

PATTERNED PAPER: Free & Breezy Kit by Anne Langpap (Two Peas in a Bucket); title paper by Katie Pertiet (Designer Digitals)

RUB-ONS: Smarshmallows Kit (Shabby Shoppe)

CHIPBOARD RINGS: By Dani Mogstadt (Designs by Dani)

STAPLES: Wonderful Kit (Shabby Shoppe)

RIBBON: By Dani Mogstadt (Design by Dani)

FONT: Impact, Pegsanna, Tuffy, Typewriter

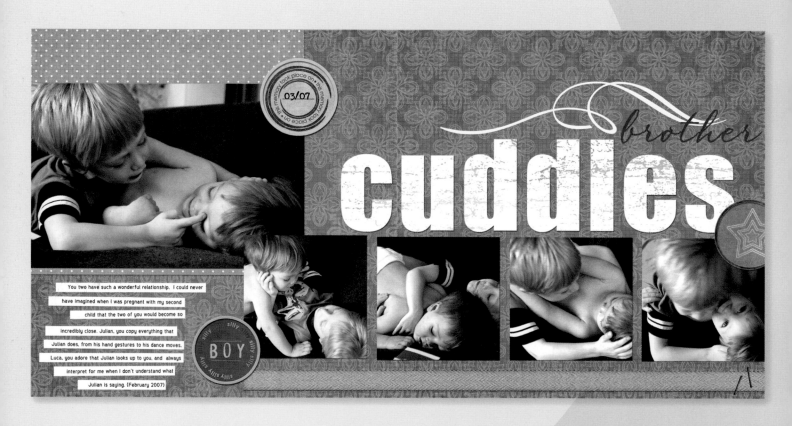

Simple Structure I wanted to include a lot of photos of my trip to the zoo with the boys, so I cropped them into different sizes and "pieced" them together. Between the photos that had "gaps," I adhered pieces of patterned paper with a suitably outdoorsy feel.

Simple Story We have a great little zoo right in the middle of Manhattan, and it's such a treat to be able to hop on the subway to go see some turtles and llamas. I don't think the boys fully understand how cool this is, but hey, they love it anyway!

Simple Technique If you're anything like me, you've amassed a bit of a ribbon collection. This is a neat way to use up some ribbon but still keep the design clean and fresh. Use a craft knife to cut a small slit in your background cardstock, and then weave the ribbon into the slit.

SUPPLIES

CARDSTOCK: Bazzill

PATTERNED PAPER: Crate Paper

STICKERS: 7gypsies, Doodlebug

RUB-ONS: Die Cuts With A View

CHIPBOARD LETTERS: Heidi Swapp

FLOWER: Doodlebug

FONTS: Marker

EYELETS, RIBBON: Unknown

ADHESIVE: Duck, Zig

SUPPLIES

CARDSTOCK: Bazzill

PATTERNED PAPER: We R Memory Keepers

RUB-ONS: Autumn Leaves, Making Memories

STICKERS: 7gypsies

DIE-CUT: QuicKutz (heart)

FONT: Kleptocracy, Modern No. 20

ADHESIVE: We R Memory Keepers, Xyron

Simple Structure If one of the less-dominant colors in your photos is black, frame them with black cardstock to really make them pop off the page.

Simple Idea Like every mom, I am often worn out by my kids. And it's hard to remember what life was like before I had them—what did I do with all that time? It took a passing comment by my sister to jolt me into recognizing how much I've changed and what that change means to me.

Simple Idea Use long phrase stickers as a border around your photos for an unusual touch.

princess hunt...

when we found out there were SIX princesses at Disneyland, we knew we were going to get all their autographs. It was quite the challenge to track them down, and took a pretty big chunk of the day, that's for sure. Towards, the end, Karl and I were phoning each other with 'princess sitting information' like Secret Service Agents! But we did

06/15/2005

Simple Structure Using squares as building blocks is an excellent way to pull together a quick, eye-catching layout. If you have photos that you don't want to crop down into squares, crop them into rectangles and they will still fit into your scheme.

Simple Story My friend Lori has the most beautiful girls, and it's clear they had a fantastic time at Disneyland hunting for princesses. If any of the princesses had been excluded from the spread, I think the girls would have hunted ME down!

Simple Technique Stitch along the edges of your main photo block to add polish, particularly when you have photos of girls to scrapbook (of course, I use stitching on my boy pages, too, and it works great!). There's that flourish shape once again. I told you it was versatile!

SUPPLIES

CARDSTOCK: Cuddlebug Kit (Shabby Shoppe)

PATTERNED PAPER: Free & Breezy Kit by Anne Langpap (Two Peas in a Bucket); Ledger Sun Prints by Katie Pertiet (Designer Digitals)

FLOURISH: By Jen Wilson (Jen Wilson Designs)

STITCHES: Spool of Stitches by Tia Bennet (Two Peas in a Bucket)

CHIPBOARD LETTERS: Silly Nut-Nut Kit (Shabby Shoppe)

RHINESTONES: By Jen Wilson (Jen Wilson Designs)

BRAD: Basic Brads by Sande Krieger (Two Peas in a Bucket)

TAG: Mega Tag Pack by Katie Pertiet (Designer Digitals)

DECORATIVE EDGES: (Shabby Shoppe)

FONT: Snappy Script Light, Tuffy

SUPPLIES

CARDSTOCK: Krafty Christmas by Christine Smith (Digi Chick)

PATTERNED PAPER: Krafty Christmas by Christine Smith (Digi Chick)

LETTERS: Stitched Black by Jen Wilson (Jen Wilson Designs)

BRUSH: Meldir Snowflakes (Internet download)

STITCHES: Spools of Stitches by Tia Bennet (Two Peas in a Bucket)

FONT: Carpenter, TW Cen MT

Simple Structure Try this block structure when you want to highlight one photo in particular. Be careful that your multi-photo page doesn't visually "outweigh" the opposite page. To avoid this, place your other elements, such as title and journaling, on the same page as your single photo.

Simple Story All of these photos are simply stunning. But it was the photo of the lit tree that really took my breath away, so I wanted to find a way to highlight it on my page.

Simple Technique Choosing elements, as well as the material they're made of, is critical to the success of the layout. Try to select elements that work well with the "feel" of your layout. On this digital page, I wanted to convey warmth and softness, so I used felt letters for the title and lots of stitching.

Simple Structure This layout really has a story to tell, so I wanted each photo to stand on its own yet be linked visually to the others. The journaling and title also fit neatly between the photos, leaving plenty of white space where the eye can rest.

Simple Story We're beginning homeschooling of my eldest in September, and I don't really know where it will lead. Sometimes I am nervous, other times excited and usually a mixture of both. When my boys were playing with the ball in the water, I was reminded of just how exciting learning can be, and, while I'm still nervous, I can safely say I am ready for the adventure to begin.

Simple Idea Sometimes you find you can easily crop your photos to a similar height, but not a similar width, or vice versa. Play with ways you might arrange your photos if they're all the same height but different widths, like I did here. How might you arrange them so that the resulting layout "works"?

SUPPLIES

CARDSTOCK: Bazzill

PATTERNED PAPER: American Crafts

BRADS: Making Memories

LETTER STICKERS: KI Memories

ACRYLIC LETTERS: Heidi Swapp

FONT: Times New Roman

ADHESIVE: We R Memory Keepers

Yellow bALL Physics

So we're at this sort of random park near Chambers Street, not a park you'd even really notice walking by it. We were just going to meet Michael there and then head over to the water with the boys. But somehow the gorgeous day made the park inviting, and the water fountain in the middle captivated the boys. We'd brought a little yellow ball with us and of course, it ended up in the water. We began to talk about how the fountain makes waves which bring the ball back to the sides. Luca and Julian threw the ball into the water, and in delight, anticipated its return to the sides so they could throw it again. It suddenly hit me how totally exciting it's going to be to homeschool Luca next year. As soon as we got home, I hopped online to finish up the homeschool research I'd begun (and never finished) last year. I can't wait til September! (4.07)

ARTWORK CREATED BY Amanda Probst

SUPPLIES

CARDSTOCK: Bazzill

PATTERNED PAPER:
American Crafts

LETTER STICKERS: American
Crafts, Creative Imaginations

METAL LETTER: American Crafts

FONT: Rockwell

ADHESIVE: Herma

Simple Structure Adhering a wide strip of patterned paper along the bottom of both pages of a two-page layout provides a grounding for the remainder of the page.

Simple Story Amanda says, "My silly middle son has so many quirks that are 'his,' and I delight in jotting them down regularly. They don't always lend themselves to accompanying pictures or layouts all to themselves, so I group them and just put it all down on one layout. I'm able to remember his funny sayings and behaviors, and he gets to see his smiling face."

Simple Idea Break up your journaling by dividing it into sections or blocks. This works well if you have a timeline you want to convey (such as a beginning, middle and end), or if you have different sections to your story.

Simple Structure I love how this layout uses bold strips of cardstock to lead your eye from left to right.

Simple Story Tracey says, "I love to scrap the little moments in life. Emily's face was so priceless in these pictures that a layout was a must, and since it was about a labeler, it made creating the journaling strips super easy!"

Simple Idea Keep your camera handy, even while you're doing mundane chores like organizing your scrap stuff. You never know when you might capture a wonderful moment.

SUPPLIES

CARDSTOCK: Bazzill, Club Scrap

RUB-ONS: Making Memories

BRADS: Making Memories

LETTER STICKERS: American Crafts

LABELER: Dymo

INK: Stampin' Up

ADHESIVE: Tombow, WeR Memory Keepers

labeler *love*

I'M SURE IT WAS MY FAULT FOR LEAVING IT ON THE FLOOR.

I WAS JUST TRYING TO ORGANIZE MY OFFICE.

BUT ONCE SHE HAD IT, THERE WAS NO GETTING IT BACK.

ARTWORK CREATED BY Tracey Odachowski

SUPPLIES

CARDSTOCK: Bazzill

PATTERNED PAPER: Chatterbox

BRADS: American Crafts

CHIPBOARD NUMBER: Heidi Swapp

CHIPBOARD CORNER: Chatterbox

STICKER: Chatterbox

ADHESIVE: Tombow

Simple Structure Create a layout using one great photo, and border the layout with two strips of patterned paper.

Simple Story Celeste says, "These photos are just a few of many great photos captured at the park on Sam's birthday. This paper line is probably my favorite. I knew the bright colors would convey the sense of playfulness I was going for. I couldn't resist enlarging the photo of Sam on "his" slide. The rest of the design fell into place from there."

Simple Idea Rather than simply snapping photos "straight on," capture them from different angles and perspectives to create a visually appealing layout.

We returned to Jonathan's Dream on your second birthday. It was the perfect place for a birthday picnic on a surprisingly warm day in November. It's amazing how much you've grown in just a few short weeks. Our last trip to the playground you were hesitant and uncoordinated. You really surprised everyone with your newfound dexterity and adventurous spirit. Climbing ladders, slipping down the slides, and scaling large tires, you did it all! I couldn't resist snapping this picture of you on Sam's Slide – so appropriate as this is where you spent the majority of your time on the playground. Happy 2nd Birthday, Sammy!

ARTWORK CREATED BY Celeste Smith

Simple Structure This layout uses an original (and unusual!) shape as its centerpiece, and the graduated sizes of the letters effectively convey a sense of energy and excitement.

Simple Story Tracey says, "Every once in a while I get ideas in my head for a title treatment, and this one seemed to fit perfectly with our pictures from the zoo."

Simple Technique Try creating an unusually shaped photo collage. There's no need to stick to boring rectangles and squares! Crop your photos into circles, diamonds or even parallelograms. (Remember those? Betcha never thought you'd use them outside of geometry class!)

SUPPLIES

CARDSTOCK: Bazzill, Stampin' Up

PATTERNED PAPER: Hambly

FONTS: Arial Black (Zoo), Blueprint

ADHESIVE: Tombow

81

Simple Structure Lining up my photos in a row across two pages was a super fast way to complete this layout. These two handcut swirls add a fun touch, while also conveying the "free wheeling" and relaxed sense of the day itself.

Simple Story This was such a weird winter! The weather was so warm on this particular day, and Julian was so excited to run around in just a sweater in the grass.

Simple Technique It's easier than it looks to create these handcut flourishes. Simply flip your cardstock over and pencil in your swirls, then cut them out. You don't even have to erase your pencil lines since they won't show on your final layout.

SUPPLIES

CARDSTOCK: Bazzill

PATTERNED PAPER: Scenic Route

RUB-ON LETTERS: American Crafts

LETTER STICKERS: Arctic Frog

FONT: TW Cen MT

FABULOUS PHOTOS

Have you ever looked at the hundreds of photos you've managed to take and wondered, "How in the world am I going to scrap all of these?" I certainly have! Here are a few photo tips to keep in mind when creating a great two-page layout:

- Vary perspective and depth. When taking photos, vary the angle at which you take them. Get some shots from down low (worm's eye view) and some from above (bird's eye view). Experiment with close-ups and long panoramic shots.

- Don't be afraid to crop your photos. Create visual interest by using a variety of sizes. Long gone are the days of only 3" x 5" (8cm x 13cm) or 4" x 6" (10cm x 15cm) formats.

- Solicit a variety of facial expressions from your photo subjects. As tricky as it may sometimes be, this is particularly important when creating a layout featuring only one person. This technique will serve as a window into their soul.

Simple Structure I actually was inspired by a Web site design for this layout. I loved the way the lines connect the photos and wanted to incorporate that into a layout.

Simple Story My son and his good friend Stan are two crazy kids, that's for sure. Their friendship is a big part of my son's life, so it was important for me to scrap it.

Simple Technique Use a pen to draw lines to connect your photos. This will not only serve as an interesting design element, it will also guide the eye across the layout.

SUPPLIES

CARDSTOCK: Bazzill

PATTERNED PAPER: SEI

RUB-ON LETTERS: Making Memories

STICKERS: Making Memories

MESH: Magic Mesh

STAMPS: Making Memories

FONT: Gilligan's Island, Tuffy

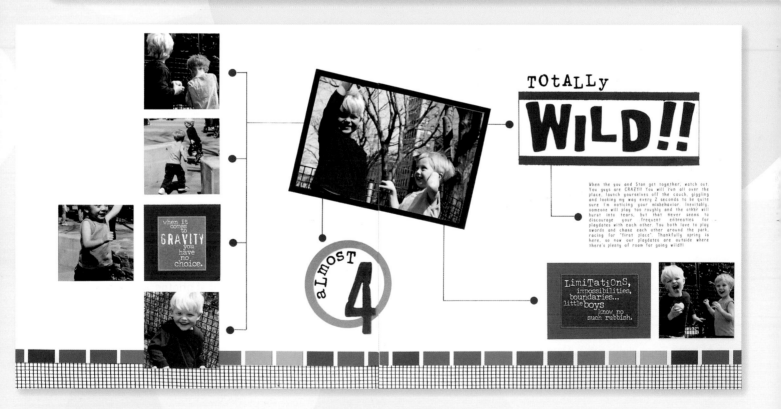

chapter five

TEXT AS A DESIGN ELEMENT

JOURNALING IS SO OFTEN RELEGATED to the end of the scrapbooking process. Some crafters say journaling upsets their layout design or balance, or they simply don't know where to fit it in after all the other elements are in place. But the text on your pages not only serves as a way to communicate your unique and personal story, it also adds to the composition of your design when integrated effectively.

Rather than viewing journaling as a chore, think of the many ways your text can enhance your layouts. Some possibilities include journaling in a unique shape or at an angle. You can wrap a photo with lines of journaling, or use colored text for a playful feel. If your layout is about visiting a duck pond, you could journal in a circle to mimic the shape of the pond. If you're scrapbooking your son's latest football victory, you could try using a variety of bold, masculine fonts set at different angles to convey movement and energy.

In this chapter you will learn how to think of journaling as an integral design element and how text can be incorporated to create a clean, simple look.

You work hard to make your business the very best it can be. But you don't think of it as 'work', not exactly. You love what you do. You have a passion, one that you've had for twenty years, a passion for art, for paintings, and for restoration. You read art catalogs for fun, spend hours in museums. I truly hope the boys find their passion, just as you have.

play

work

How do you measure the important things in life?

You have never been much of a snow fan. Come to think of it, you've never been much of a cold fan, a wind fan, or an ice fan. You always liked the way snow looked—from the inside of our cozy apartments. But once you got outside, forget it. Wailing and crying immediately ensued. On this day, however, things were different. The day was sunny and bright and windless. And for the first time ever, you *really* enjoyed the snow (Luca, February 2005)

Simple Structure This layout uses handcut curves to convey movement and excitement.

Simple Story It is a rare day when we have just the right combination of snow and mild weather. I was so glad to have my camera with me because, seriously, this type of day comes along once in a blue moon.

Simple Technique Use journaling strips of different lengths to add liveliness and energy to your layout.

SUPPLIES

CARDSTOCK: Bazzill

PATTERNED PAPER: KI Memories

RUB-ONS: KI Memories

LETTER STICKERS: SEI

FONT: Traditionell Sans

PEN: Sakura

ADHESIVE: Duck

Simple Structure Don't be afraid to leave white space on two-page layouts. You might say, "Hey, there are only three photos on this layout, why not make it a one-pager?" Or, "Put some more photos on there!" Well, I really wanted to convey a sense of openess, or "end-lessness" in this layout. And since the background cardstock matches the sand so well, it gives the layout a feeling of never-ending beach.

Simple Story I am a beach bum, and, thankfully, my children are too. There is nothing like spending endless summer days playing on the beach. Nothing.

Simple Technique Use long journaling strips to make a border for your cardstock. If you don't have a wide-format printer, just print the strips as wide as you can and lay them side-by-side.

SUPPLIES

CARDSTOCK: Bazzill

PAPER: We R Memory Keepers

CHIPBOARD: We R Memory Keepers

RUB-ONS: Die Cuts With A View

FONT: Arial Narrow, Impact

ADHESIVE: Duck, Xyron

We live right in the heart of downtown Manhattan near Battery Park City. We moved here from the Upper East Side a couple of years ago, right before I gave birth to Julian. I love our apartment. We have a view of the Statue of Liberty and the water, we have a washing machine and dryer (in the apartment no less!!!) and the boys love the playroom on the 2nd floor, where they can go nuts and make a big mess.

Transportation in NYC basically involves taking the subway or riding in an expensive, lurching cab. I much prefer the subway; $2 (as of January 2007) gets you basically anywhere in NYC, and usually in under 45 minutes. Of course, there is the small matter of lugging the stroller up and down the stairs, and the impenetrable summer heat in the stations. But other than that, the subway's the way to go.

Oh, another plus of the subway that I almost forgot to mention: performers. Dancers, singers, guitarists, drummers... they all congregate in the subways to strut their stuff and hope for a lucky break. Sometimes, I do wish for silence. But other times, the performance is so moving, or invigorating, that I am happy I paused for a moment to watch. And I drop a dollar in the outstretched hat as they pass by.

the Big Apple

Living in NYC is invigorating, exhausting, frustrating, expensive, noisy, rushed, stressful, exciting and it never ends. There are times, I admit, when I want to leave and move to a farm in Vermont (no, really.) But for the time being at least, this is where we are. This is the only home my boys have known. This is where I grew up, this is where Michael grew up, and this is the place we call home.

One thing that stinks about the city is the ridiculous cost of owning a car. It would be nice to be able to drive out of the city in our own car once in a while. Buying the car isn't really the problem...it's the parking. Do you SEE what it costs to park in the city??? $591 a month and that doesn't even include the 20% tax. Even if we had the money to spare, I doubt we could justify it. Heck, that's alot of scrapbook supplies, know what i mean? And parking on the street is crazzzzzzzzy.

Up to 2 hrs 22.01
Up to 10 hrs 30.41
Max to 24 hrs 38.01
Vans add'l 8.45
Mthly Rate 591.35
Main floor add'l 50.69
O'sized veh. add'l 50.69

There aren't enough good things that I can say about Little Mish. This place has nurtured Luca since he was two years old. Three days a week, Luca has gone to Little Mish, and been cared for by Eileen, Willie, Blanca, Jennifer, and Elaine. He's been allowed to develop in his own way, on his own direction without judgement and with a ton of support and fun. When Luca comes back home next year, Julian will begin his first year.

THE LITTLE MISSIONARY'S DAY NURSERY

Living downtown does mean we live in the shadow of the tragedy of 9/11. Every day, we walk by the hole in the ground where the World Trade Center used to be. And this is hard. For the first few months of living here, I tried to block it out. I mean, we walked by it every day, and I wasn't really ready to acknowledge its profound presence. But lately, I take a moment, even just a breath, to remember what happened here six years ago.

The parks for the kids in Battery Park City are like no other in New York. They're managed by the BPC Parks Association, which really is on the ball. Toys are put out daily for the kids to play with (and good ones! not ratty broken toys...) They organize toddler tumbling classes, art classes, yoga for teens and fishing lessons. The parks themselves have water sprinklers, gorgeous art and really well-designed jungle gyms. Oh, and don't forget rubber matting!

SUPPLIES

CARDSTOCK: Bazzill

FONT: Elementary SF, Unicorn

ADHESIVE: 3L, Xyron

Simple Structure Using a grid is a fun and easy way to display photos from different locations or time periods.

Simply Story I love living in Manhattan. OK, sometimes the noise and the crowds drive me a little bonkers, but overall I am still firmly on the pro-NYC side of the fence. I wanted to create a layout that shows all the things, both big and small, that comprise our day-to-day life here in New York City.

Simple Idea Even if you don't have a wide format printer, you can easily re-create the look of this layout by printing your journaling in square text boxes. Use a square punch to punch out your journaling and adhere to your background.

...you are my
BRIGHT STAR

Simple Structure Try using an unusual shape for your text to draw your reader in. This shape can even be the underpinning for the entire layout rather than an "add-on" at the end. For this layout, I printed the journaling first, and then added the other elements around it.

Simple Story I wanted to express to my son a bit about why he's so special to me.

Simple Idea Use your layout to tell a story to your child about what makes him or her so unique. Be very specific when describing his or her special qualities.

SUPPLIES

CARDSTOCK: Bazzill

BRADS: Queen & Co.

RUB-ON LETTERS: Imagination Project

PAPER FRILLS: Doodlebug

FONTS: Good Girl, Steelfish

ADHESIVE: 3L, Xyron, Zig

Toothbrush Bandit

GOOD TIMES

Just about every morning, when Papa gets ready to brush his teeth, he yells "Hey, where'd my toothbrush go?" The inevitable toothbrush hunt ensues. See, the thing is, when I take my morning shower after Papa's gone, just about the only thing that will keep you happy and occupied for those all-too-brief ten minutes are mama and papa's toothbrushes. You stand near the sink, pointing plaintively at our toothbrushes, and of course, I relent. You sometimes will stay in the bathroom, but have been known to wander into the living room and hide them in the bookshelf. (December 2006)

Simple Structure Two intersecting circles provide the basis for this fun and lively layout.

Simple Story My youngest son, Julian, went through a crazy obsession with toothbrushes—I mean CRAZY. He took those toothbrushes everywhere. How could I not document that?

Simple Idea Place your title along a curve to create an interesting perspective. Die-cut letters or sticker letters make it easy to arrange.

SUPPLIES

CARDSTOCK: Bazzill

PATTERNED PAPER: Autumn Leaves

LETTER STICKERS: Arctic Frog

STICKERS: 7gypsies

FONT: Mammagamma

ADHESIVE: 3L, Xyron

Simple Structure A circle is a fantastic building block for a layout. Try placing your text within a circle at the center of your page and build the remainder of the elements around it.

Simple Story Luca and his friend Stan have been friends since they turned four years old. I've often wondered who my earliest friends were and what my relationship was like with them. When Luca grows up, all he'll have to do is look at this layout!

Simple Technique Journaling in a circle is quite easy with the use of image-editing software.

SUPPLIES

CARDSTOCK: Shabby Princess (Shabby Shoppe)

RUB-ONS: Shabby Princess (Shabby Shoppe)

FONT: Basic Sans Light SF, Impact

Luca and Stan, the two of you definitely have a special relationship. First of all, the two of you look like brothers. With your blonde hair and neverending giggles and screams, it's no wonder people think you're related. We meet up with Stan and his mom Sarah just about every Friday for a playdate, and the two of you are go go go until Sarah and I decide to break up the party about 3 hours later. Whether it's heading to the park, or just playing at each other's houses, the two of you always have a great time together. On this day, the day was luckily warm enough to head out to the playground. You jointly decided to dig a huge hole, and when snack time came, you took turns "watching over" the hole to make sure none of the younger kids ruined it. (3/07)

uncle whit & aunt mimi

I actually managed to grab my camera and snap some shots when Uncle Whit andyour (almost) Aunt Mimi came over to take you and Julian out for pizza the other day. Whit definitely gets the "right" way to rough-house with you...can't wait for you two to have your own (Hint, hint!)

January 2007

SUPPLIES

CARDSTOCK: By Shannon Lee (My Digital Muse)

TAG: Classic Kraft Labels by Tia Bennet (Two Peas in a Bucket)

FONT: Bebas, Century Gothic, Impact, Susie's Hand

CHIPBOARD: Atomic Cupcake (Atomic Cupcake)

TITLE ALPHABET: Dani Mogstad (Sweet Shoppe Designs)

Simple Structure I really wanted this layout to match the playful mood of the photos. To add this sense of fun, I placed them at an angle for a lighthearted feel.

Simple Story Luca is absolutely enamored with Whitten and Mimi, and I managed to capture these candid shots during a recent visit.

Simple Technique It's easy to "fit" your text into an unusually shaped area, like the angled area next to the photos in this layout. Simply use your space bar! (Admit it, you thought it was some complicated computer thing, right?)

Simple Structure Three circular photos surrounded by a larger circle cut out of patterned paper form the basis of this energetic layout.

Simple Story My youngest son is intrepid (although not as much as my oldest son). It took a bit of encouragement to get Julian to try the slide on his own, and, like any good scrapbooker, I had my camera ready to capture the moment.

Simple Technique Journaling in a circle is a fun and interesting way to easily add visual appeal to your layout.

SUPPLIES

CARDSTOCK: Bazzill

PATTERNED PAPER: Die Cuts With A View

RUB-ONS: Die Cuts With A View

FONT: Franklin Gothic Demi Condensed, Lacuna Regular

ADHESIVE: 3L

TYPE DESIGN

Here are some simple and fun ways to arrange text:

- In a circle
- As a column
- In a wave shape
- As lines bordering your photograph
- Sideways
- In journaling strips
- Cutting individual words out of cardstock
- Hugging the edge of a curved piece of cardstock

SUPPLIES

CARDSTOCK: Kraft by Suzy Nunes
(Sweet Shoppe Designs)

SHABBY ACCENTS: Princess
Organic Kit (Shabby Shoppe)

STITCHES: Spool of Stitches by Tia
Bennett (Two Peas in a Bucket)

FONT: ScholBroadway

Simple Structure I really wanted this layout to reflect the elegant softness of a fall day and was inspired by an ad I saw that had curved photos.

Simple Story My friend Jennifer's daughter is such a cutie, and I wanted to create a special layout as a gift for her.

Simple Idea Place your text along the edge of a curve in your layout by placing just one or two words on a line. This idea works best if you're using either a poem, or simple descriptive words/ phrases for your journaling.

You work hard to make your business the very best it can be. But you don't think of it as 'work', not exactly. You love what you do. You have a passion, one that you've had for twenty years, a passion for art, for paintings, and for restoration. You read art catalogs for fun, spend hours in museums. I truly hope the boys find their passion, just as you have.

How do you measure the important things in life?

work play

Simple Structure Try placing your title at an unusual angle. Because I was comparing and contrasting the two aspects of "work" and "play," I placed each word of the title at an angle.

Simple Story My husband's work is so much more to him than just a way to earn money. It is something he is deeply passionate about, and he brings all his energy, love and dedication to it.

Simple Idea Is there some aspect of your life that has "two sides" that you could translate into a layout? How about "mother/wife" or "woman/mother" or "child/adult"? In what ways are you both and how do you integrate the two?

SUPPLIES

CARDSTOCK: Bazzill

PATTERNED PAPER: Daisy D's

BRADS: American Crafts

PEN: American Crafts

METAL: Jo-Ann Stores

LETTER STICKERS: Chatterbox

RUB-ONS: Daisy D's

FONT: Lacuna Reg, Rockwell

BRADS: Creative Xpress

Kashmir 1976

When we were young girls (I was 6 and my sister Kelly was 10) my parents took us on a trip around the world. We went to India and Kenya and Turkey and Egypt and Sri Lanka. I remember snippets of the trip (I'm one of those people who doesn't have a good recollection of pretty much anything prior to age 10). I remember the oppressive heat in Africa and I remember the Sphinx in Egypt. I remember my brother nearly slipping into a crevice while we were exploring the Egyptian pyramids. I remember riding donkeys up a mountain (Turkey? my memory fails me) And now that I am a parent, I look back with wonder that my parents would even consider undertaking such a trip with two young girls...I get stressed just going to Long Island with my boys! We were gone for over three months-- imagine the packing! Anyway, I am grateful that my parents took us on this trip at such a young age. Who knows-maybe it was the spark that led me to have such a fascination with other cultures throughout my life? Maybe it's what led me to major in Cultural Anthropology in college. Right now, Kashmir is not a safe place to travel due to civil war, and I'm glad I had a chance to visit it when I did. (journaling 4/07)

Simple Structure The column of text is the defining design element in this ultra-simple layout.

Simple Story I came across this photo of my mother, my sister and me taken when we traveled during my childhood and was immediately flooded with memories. I quickly jotted them down and included them on this simple layout.

Simple Idea Remember to scrapbook yourself as a child. We all have at least a few photos of ourselves from when we were children. If you don't want to scrap the original photo, scan it to make a copy and work with that.

SUPPLIES

CARDSTOCK: Kraft by Suzy Nunes (Sweet Shoppe Designs)

STITCHES: Spool of Stitches by Tia Bennet (Two Peas in a Bucket)

BRAD: Basic Brads by Sande Krieger (Two Peas in a Bucket)

FONT: Typewriter Old Style, Yanone Kaffeesatz

Simple Structure The oversized circle of patterned paper on this fun layout immediately grabs your eye, and the funny journaling truly captures the special moment between Tracey's son and her husband.

Simple Story Tracey says, "Sometimes I think my husband is a bigger kid than my son. The way they play together is truly magical. What a pair of goofballs!"

Simple Technique Create a wavy filmstrip of photos by cropping your photos in graduated sizes.

SUPPLIES

CARDSTOCK: Bazzill

PATTERNED PAPER: Autumn Leaves

LETTER STICKERS: Chatterbox

STAR PUNCH: Family Treasures

FONT: Bernhard Mod BT

June 26, 2005 – This reporter was able to take a rare glimpse inside the secret lair of two superhero kin. Otherwise known as DynoDad and SuperGabe, These men have been fighting crime together for nearly five years.

Their latest achievement was seen earlier this morning when, in a few minutes time, DynoDad was assisted by his trusty sidekick in cleaning the playroom. It was a feat like no other I had seen. I was impressed by their speed, which, for the most part, could not be caught on film. But I was fortunate enough to catch one photo of the swift SuperGabe in action. Look at the motion! It is poetry!

When they were done, they were kind enough to pose for me for a few seconds to take some more photos for their adoring public. Such a generous act for two busy fellows. And, before I knew it, they were off again to save the house as we know it!

ARTWORK CREATED BY Tracey Odachowski

Simple Structure What I love about this layout is how the angle really draws you in. The linear array of rectangular word boxes on the left lends color and fun to the layout, but it's the story that keeps your attention.

Simple Story Amanda says, "I remember distinctly one morning during summer swim lessons when my husband came with us to watch the boys. Afterwards, as we were walking back to the car, my husband laughed and noted how Asher hurried to get to his 'side.' I smiled and told him I should do a layout about that. A week or so later my husband took this picture so I could do just that."

Simple Technique Use image-editing software to create an interesting journaling shape. Alternatively, simply use your own handwriting. Pull out your handy ruler and pencil to create journaling lines; then simply erase them once your ink has dried.

SUPPLIES

CARDSTOCK: Bazzill

FONTS: Century Gothic, Kravitz, Rockwell Extra Bold, Texas Hero

ADHESIVE: Herma

JUMP FOR JUSTIFICATION

One simple way to change the look of your layout is to change the text justification. Fully justified text is probably my favorite easy way to add a clean, sharp look to any scrapbook page. Left or right justified text can help direct the eye towards different parts of the layout. Having a "ragged edge" to one side of the journaling can serve an artistic purpose as well, allowing you to add more visual weight to one side or to simply experiment with a more relaxed approach to text arrangement.

ARTWORK CREATED BY Amanda Probst

PHOTO TAKEN BY Nathan Probst

Simple Structure The curve in this layout is unusual and fresh, yet it doesn't distract from the wonderful story.

Simple Story Celeste says, "Graphic design can be found all around us and provides great inspiration for our books. This particular layout was based on an advertisement. It took a bit of time to get the pieces of the circle to match up and to stagger the journaling so that it printed along the curve, but the effect is really wonderful."

Simple Idea Take photos of your child's close friends and scrap about their relationship. When grown, your child will treasure these tidbits from when he or she was young.

SUPPLIES

CARDSTOCK: Bazzill

PATTERNED PAPER: Pixel Decor

BRADS: American Crafts

PEN: American Crafts

METAL: Jo-Ann Stores

ALPHABET STICKERS: Chatterbox

the gang

You absolutely adore our neighbors, Jack and Emma. Just like Adam you stand at the front door and yell across the street to them. You've spent many spring and summer evenings playing in the Tapia's front yard. Basically, you chase the other kids around, trying desperately to keep up. I'll be sad when we move next year, we'll lose touch with these friends. We'll have to make special visits back so the Brunswick Ave. Gang can reunite and enjoy each other's company once more.

Adam, Jack, Emma and You
May 2005

ARTWORK CREATED BY Celeste Smith

Journaling translation: For some time you've been passionate about the small notes that you scatter here and there all around the house. It always starts with a small drawing, then as you don't yet know how to write on your own, you ask us to write for you. These small notes are for Dad and Mum, and they all say just about the same thing: "I love you." It's utterly charming to find these notes on our door or beside our bed! And I want to tell you that we love you, too.

Mr. post it

Depuis quelque temps tu te passionnes | pour les petits mots que tu parsèmes

de-ci de-là dans toute la maison. | ça commence toujours | par un petit dessin

Puis comme tu ne sais pas encore | écrire tout seul, tu nous demandes d'écrire à ta place.

Ces petits mots il y en a pour papa et pour maman,

Et ils disent tous à peu près la même chose : | "Je t'aime "

C'est totalement charmant de retrouver | ces post-it sur notre porte ou à côté de notre lit !

et je voudrais te dire que nous aussi on t'aime.

ARTWORK CREATED BY Severine Di Giacomo

SUPPLIES

CARDSTOCK: Bazzill

PATTERNED PAPER: American Crafts

LETTER STICKERS: American Crafts

STAR SHAPE: Quickutz

FONT: Tw Cen MT

ADHESIVE: 3M

Simple Structure This layout showcases one great photo and a lovely expanse of patterned paper. By breaking up the journaling strips into small clusters, Severine mimics the very activity she is journaling about.

Simple Story Severine says, "I don't want to forget these cute, little everyday moments so that's why I love to document them. Here, the journaling strips remind me of the small papers that we found scattered in our house."

Simple Idea Using journaling strips is a quick and easy way to tell your story. Simply print your journaling on cardstock, leaving enough room between each line to cut with a trimmer. After cutting the strips apart, adhere them to your layout.

Simple Structure This is such a playful layout. By placing the two photos of her children in opposing corners, Tracey allows each to have a unique place in this special family story.

Simple Story Tracey says, "Seeing my children hanging upside down brought back such fond memories of my childhood. It thrilled me to make this connection to my past."

Simple Technique Handcutting an unusual title like this might take a bit of time, but it's well worth the effort.

SUPPLIES

CARDSTOCK: Bazzill, Club Scrap

PATTERNED PAPER: KI Memories

PHOTO CORNERS: KI Memories

FONT: Arial Black

ADHESIVE: Tombow

My dad used to hang me upside down by my feet as a kid. It was one of my favorite things, and one of my fondest memories. Now, I'm 25 years older, and I get to do it with my kids. The first time I held one of you upside down, you were both hooked. Now, Daddy gets to do it, and I snap pictures. Even Emily wants to do it, and screams bloody murder when we have to put her down.

upside down

Gabe is fine with taking turns, but Emily hates it. The entire time it is his turn, she stands at Chris' feet screaming. I have to admit, it is pretty hilarious to watch. But I'm glad that I get to share one of my favorite things with them.

ARTWORK CREATED BY Tracey Odachowski

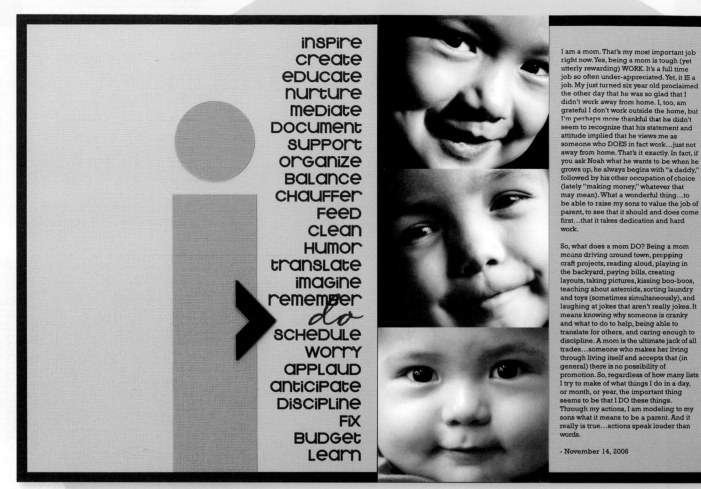

inspire
create
educate
nurture
mediate
document
support
organize
balance
chauffer
feed
clean
humor
translate
imagine
remember
do
schedule
worry
applaud
anticipate
discipline
fix
budget
learn

I am a mom. That's my most important job right now. Yes, being a mom is tough (yet utterly rewarding) WORK. It's a full time job so often under-appreciated. Yet, it IS a job. My just turned six year old proclaimed the other day that he was so glad that I didn't work away from home. I, too, am grateful I don't work outside the home, but I'm perhaps more thankful that he didn't seem to recognize that his statement and attitude implied that he views me as someone who DOES in fact work...just not away from home. That's it exactly. In fact, if you ask Noah what he wants to be when he grows up, he always begins with "a daddy," followed by his other occupation of choice (lately "making money," whatever that may mean). What a wonderful thing...to be able to raise my sons to value the job of parent, to see that it should and does come first...that it takes dedication and hard work.

So, what does a mom DO? Being a mom means driving around town, prepping craft projects, reading aloud, playing in the backyard, paying bills, creating layouts, taking pictures, kissing boo-boos, teaching about asteroids, sorting laundry and toys (sometimes simultaneously), and laughing at jokes that aren't really jokes. It means knowing why someone is cranky and what to do to help, being able to translate for others, and caring enough to discipline. A mom is the ultimate jack of all trades...someone who makes her living through living itself and accepts that (in general) there is no possibility of promotion. So, regardless of how many lists I try to make of what things I do in a day, or month, or year, the important thing seems to be that I DO these things. Through my actions, I am modeling to my sons what it means to be a parent. And it really is true...actions speak louder than words.

- November 14, 2006

ARTWORK CREATED BY Amanda Probst

Simple Structure By lining the important words of her journaling along the right edge of the left page of this layout, Amanda created a striking and gorgeous layout describing what she does in a day.

Simple Story Amanda says, "This layout is all about the journaling and is one of those that just touches my heart every time I look at it, knowing that this is the kind of thing I'm going to want to remember and be remembered by."

Simple Idea Do you have important stories from your life that you'd like to share, but don't have specific photos to match them? In this case, Amanda simply chose three photos of her boys that she loved, and the journaling became the focus.

SUPPLIES

CARDSTOCK: Bazzill, Prism

FONTS: Kravitz, Pegsanna, Rockwell

Simple Structure I moved the focus of this layout off to the side to allow for the flourish along the left. I actually think the flourish looks a bit like a cat tail! I really wanted these photos to pop, so I used a light blue background. In doing so, Sunday's black fur didn't get lost.

Simple Story Sunday has been with me through it all, but until now I've never devoted a layout just to her. After 15 years, I decided it was about time.

Simple Idea If you want to emphasize certain words in your journaling, there's no need to settle for just plain black or white text. Highlight the important words by converting them to different colors. In this case, I chose colors that matched the patterned paper strip along the right side.

SUPPLIES

CARDSTOCK: Naturally Krafty Cardstock by Katie Pertiet (Designer Digitals)

STRIPE ACCENT: Apron String by Leora Sanford (Designer Digitals)

BRAD: Brad Bonanza by Pattie Knox (Designer Digitals)

SWIRL: Hipster Plumes by Anna Aspnes (Designer Digitals)

FONTS: Snappy Script Light, Symphony (Internet downloads)

What can I say? I'm ashamed to say this is the first layout I've ever done about you. And you've been in my life for... let's see... 15 years. Yep, you've lived through graduate school in Vermont, a tiny apartment in Hell's Kitchen, countless trips to Long Island to visit my mom. You were through at least five teary breakups. You've patiently and kindly put up with the innumerable stray animals that I brought home through the years. And then, of course, I had my boys, and you were relegated to a second priority in my life. And for that I am sorry. You are very special to me. You don't mind when Julian hugs too tightly. You patiently remind me when I forget to fill your bowl with fresh water (and yes, I will try not to forget the ice cubes...) You are a pretty cat: mellow and calm, you love to sleep on my neck at night. I just wanted to say thanks, Sunday, for being such a wonderful companion to me, and to my family, for all these years. (journaling written 08/26/07)

FONT FANATIC

I am a font junkie and have probably collected over 1,200 fonts since I began scrapbooking. But the truth is that I have a folder of my "most used" fonts, and I usually end up using one of them! They include Traditionell Sans, Tw CenMT, Rockwell, Pegsanna, Arial, Century Gothic and Wendy Medium. By having these "go-to" fonts, I don't spend endless hours searching for the "perfect font," because these look good every time!

chapter six

UTILIZING WHITE SPACE

WHITE SPACE IS CONSIDERED to be the area of a layout that is untouched, or "empty." An example would be an area of cardstock with no embellishments or patterned paper. White space is not purposeless space. It serves a key role in balancing all the "non-empty" space on the layout, and without it a page can look overloaded. White space also allows the viewer's eye to focus on the photos and elements without distraction.

I know there are some people who feel that "white space equals wasted space." But think about a gorgeous painting placed on an expanse of a long white wall. Wouldn't that be striking? Wouldn't your eye be drawn right to that painting, and might you not appreciate that painting even more because its display is so spectacular and clean? In fact, one of the reasons that advertisers use white space in advertisements is to convey a sense of dramatic elegance, and to focus the reader's eye on the product they're trying to sell. These lessons can definitely be applied to scrapbook layouts.

Layouts with lots of white space work best when featuring a great photo or set of photos, or when you have a real story to tell. So if you have a very special photo that you really want to showcase, or a wonderful story to share, try creating a layout with a fair amount of white space. Your resulting layout might make you appreciate that "nothing" definitely adds something!

sugar high*

and next comes the crash

BEACH *love*

You and the beach are a perfect fit. You are ALWAYS cold, so going to the beach, and hanging out in just your undies and a tee on a hot summer day is pretty much the definition of bliss to you. You walk along the shore, finding "treasure", dip your toes (barely) in the ocean, and basically enjoy yourself completely. Even better is when Papa remembers to bring the kite. Then the two of you go crazy trying to get the damn thing up in the air. It's pretty hysterical. I love that you are a beach bum, just like your mom. (Summer 2005)

SUPPLIES

CARDSTOCK: Bazzill

PATTERNED PAPER: My Mind's Eye

CUTTING TOOL: Xyron Wishblade

PENS: Sakura

FLOWER: Prima

RUB-ONS: 7gypsies, American Crafts

FONTS: Bebas, Century Gothic

ADHESIVE: We R Memory Keepers, Zig

Simple Structure When arranging a mini collage of photos, try interspersing them with small embellishments and strips of cardstock or patterned paper. By keeping all the elements within the block, the clean sense of white space is maintained.

Simple Story These giggly photos of my son perfectly captured his love of the beach.

Simple Idea Don't be afraid to mix color and black-and-white photos on the same layout. In this instance, I chose the photo I wanted to highlight and kept it in color, and converted the other two to black and white.

Simple Structure This layout uses a unique series of dots to lead into the journaling. The primary colors highlight the boyish playfulness of the photo.

Simple Story Sometimes you come across that one photo in your collection that speaks volumes. In this case, I had captured this quintessential shot of my son and immediately wanted to create a quick layout that mentioned all his favorite superheroes.

Simple Idea Journal along an edge using short, descriptive words. Don't worry about using complete sentences. Write down the first words that come to mind when you look at the photo. Don't overthink it!

SUPPLIES

CARDSTOCK: Bazzill

PATTERNED PAPER: KI Memories

FONT: TW Cen MT

RUB-ON: KI Memories

ADHESIVE: Duck

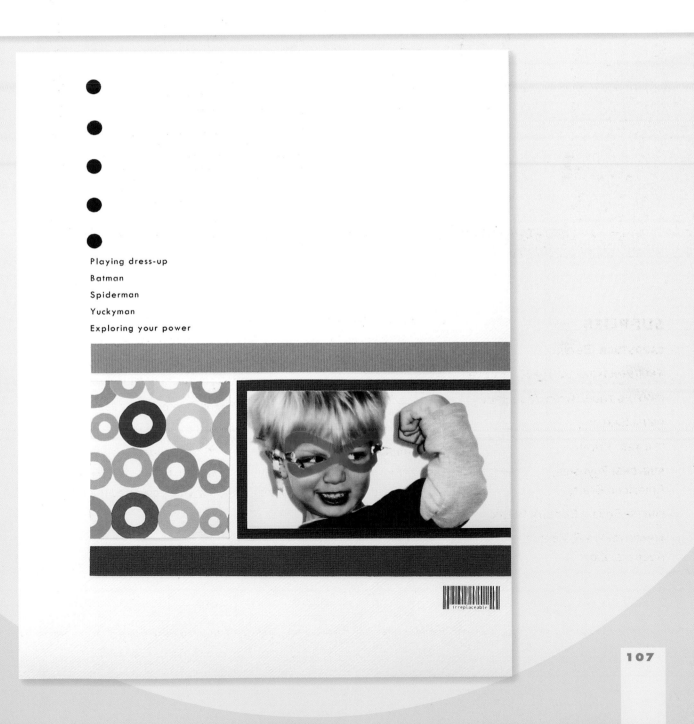

Playing dress-up

Batman

Spiderman

Yuckyman

Exploring your power

SUPPLIES

CARDSTOCK: Bazzill

PATTERNED PAPER: CherryArte

RUB-ONS: Autumn Leaves

FONT: Bullet Balls (5), District Thin, Mistral

CUTTING TOOL: Xyron Wishblade

ADHESIVE: Duck, Xyron

Simple Structure To use white space effectively, the rest of the layout must really grab the viewer and tell a story—either through the journaling or the photos. In this instance, I snapped a photo of myself and then journaled about five simple, special things in my life.

Simple Story This layout was created for an online challenge to scrap five things in life that matter most to you.

Simple Idea As scrapbookers, we're so busy documenting life around us that we tend to neglect our own perspective on our own lives. Come out from behind the camera and turn inward to think about the things that matter to you. Then record these expressions on your scrapbook pages.

listen.

There is no secret. There is no magical moment in life where you "get it", a moment when you suddenly realize you're an adult and all the things that confused you when you were a child suddenly make sense. That moment never arrives. Not when you're 10, not when you're 30. What does happen is this: everyday, you get to know yourself a little better. You (slowly) stop obsessing over every little thing. And you realize there is no big picture, there are only small moments that make up the whole. Just thought I'd let you know now.

Simple Structure A two-page layout with a significant amount of white space creates a great impact. Place your photos on one page and the title and journaling on the other page to evoke a thoughtful mood. Use colors that complement this subdued feeling.

Simple Story On this layout, I wanted to express to my son that in life there will always be questions; you will never feel like you know everything; and the only important thing is appreciating and living in the moment. If you wait until you know the "answers" to live your life, you'll be waiting a very, very long time.

Simple Technique Use image-editing software to create a border or mat around your photo.

SUPPLIES

CARDSTOCK: Bazzill

PATTERNED PAPER: We R Memory Keepers

RUB-ONS: 7gypsies

FONT: District Thin

ADHESIVE: 3L, Xyron

From: **me** To: **you**

Luca and Julian, I just wanted to tell you a few things about me that might help you out when trying to navigate this map called Mom. I am just a little bit moody (oh! you didn't know that about me?) but I can be placated by hugs. If you let me have a cup of coffee before your onslaught of morning questions and demands, I will be *much* more accomodating. Luca: when I am scrapbooking, I love it when you ask if you can help. Julian: your singing random songs as you walk around the house with Luca's underwear on your head (yes, you really do think it's a hat) can make the crappiest day golden. I appreciate those brief moments when you play trains together in your room so I can check my email. Finally, I know I get irritable when I am tired, so please, tell me to get to bed earlier. Even a mom needs a friendly reminder about the important things in life.

SUPPLIES

CARDSTOCK: Bazzill

PATTERNED PAPER: Sassafras Lass

BRADS: Queen & Co.

FONTS: District Thin, Pegsanna, Suede

ADHESIVE: 3L, Xyron

Simple Structure Sometimes it's so nice to not overthink your layouts—just jot down the ever-important journaling and adhere your photo along with a small personal touch like the brad flourish on this layout. Keep all the elements gathered together to allow for an expanse of white space over the rest of the layout. This lends a sharp, clean "edge" and a timeless look.

Simple Story I wanted to write a letter to my sons about some of my quirks and "requirements" as a mother—things that might make their lives a little bit easier when putting up with me.

Simple Idea Are there things about yourself you'd like to share with your kids? I urge you to record them in your scrapbooks. If nothing else, it might help your children better understand themselves when they get older and become parents.

Simple Structure I used a pencil and large pot lid to outline this large semicircular curve (putting the pot to good use!). The angled cut of the patterned paper directs the viewer's eye up to the photo and story. Notice how the clean white area on the left is balanced by the open space on the right. All the critical elements are tucked in one rectangular area lending an elegant, refreshing look to the layout.

Simple Story I wanted to document my son's relationship with one of his first friends. He doesn't get to see this friend as much anymore; looking back, I am so glad I took the time to document this special friendship.

Simple Technique Why not create your title out of patterned paper? Simply print your title in reverse on the back of the patterned paper, and use scissors or a sharp craft knife to cut it out.

SUPPLIES

CARDSTOCK: Bazzill

PATTERNED PAPER: Scenic Route

RUB-ONS: K&Co.

PEN: Sakura

FONT: Suede, Traditionell Sans

FLOWER: Prima

ADHESIVE: Duck, Xyron

For the first 2 years of your life, Chester was your most frequent companion. He lived just 4 blocks away, and his mom, Jen, and I became friends just a couple of weeks after you both were born. You two are quite different: you like swords and superheroes, Chester prefers reading and Thomas trains. But somehow it works. Although we've since moved downtown to Battery Park and are a subway ride away from Chester, I hope you don't grow apart. (written 06/13/06)

SUPPLIES

CARDSTOCK: Bazzill

PATTERNED PAPER: Chatterbox

RUB-ONS: Autumn Leaves

STICKERS: Chatterbox, Doodlebug, KI Memories

ADHESIVE: 3M, Xyron

Simple Structure The oval on this page adds a unique touch, while the punched doodles add a sense of playfulness. On this layout, I decided to add only one small, cropped photo placed slightly off center. Sometimes one photo will perfectly capture the emotion or story you are trying to share. In fact, this is one of the rare instances I didn't want any journaling to clutter the surrounding white space.

Simple Story All babies have their odd little habits. Julian's was to roll back on one elbow when he lay on his stomach. I just love capturing these small moments; they definitely provide the bulk of my layout content!

Simple Technique Use a hole punch to add doodles or swirls to your layout. Adhere leftover scraps of colored cardstock underneath the background for a burst of color.

Simple Structure Three square photos provide the basis for this simple cardstock layout. The harmonious colors of blue and chocolate brown serve to enhance the theme of boyish enjoyment in a sweet chocolate dessert.

Simple Story My son loves sweets, and I caught him enjoying his second piece of cake while at a recent birthday party. These aren't the best shots, so I cropped them to focus on my son and his cake.

Simple Technique Use a white gel pen and a ruler to create a sharp outline on dark paper. Place your photos off center and leave a broad area of your background untouched to create a striking visual effect.

SUPPLIES

CARDSTOCK: Bazzill

LETTER STICKERS: 7gypsies, American Crafts

PEN: Sakura

FLOWER: We R Memory Keepers

ADHESIVE: Duck, Xyron

big brother

You will always be the big brother. Watch out for Julian and keep him safe.

Simple Structure Leaving white space on your layout conveys a sense of drama and importance. The soft, muted colors allow the gentle story of two brothers to shine.

Simple Story My oldest son, Luca, is incredibly protective of his younger brother Julian. He watches out for him, helps him off the bed, takes off his shoes when we come home, and puts toothpaste on his toothbrush. I wanted him to know that I appreciate him so much.

Simple Idea Ground your main elements with the edge of your layout by using a strip of ribbon or patterned paper. This is an easy way to add a sense of spaciousness.

SUPPLIES

CARDSTOCK: Backpack Essentials Paper Kit by Kathy Moore (Scrapbook Graphics), Cabana White by Katie Pertiet (Designer Digitals)

STITCHING: Spool of Stitches by Tia Bennett (Two Peas in a Bucket)

FONT: District Thin, Typewriter New Roman

ADDITIONAL SUPPLIES: Winter Chic Kit (Shabby Shoppe)

Simple Structure White space and a cropped photo of me looking off the page create a sense of distance. A photo like this one can be especially effective when you are trying to convey a sense of lost time.

Simple Story I wanted to create a layout about the many aspects of "me," and I realized much of what I had considered an integral part of who I was lay in the past.

Simple Technique Use a digital brush to create an interesting frame on your layout.

SUPPLIES

CARDSTOCK: Bazzill

SNAPS: Making Memories

CHIPBOARD LETTERS: Heidi Swapp

RUB-ONS: Luxe Designs

FONT: District Thin

DIGITAL BRUSH: By Jason Gaylor (Designfruit)

then

singer
marathon runner
horse freak
Club Med tennis instructor
world traveller
investment banker
Yalie
yoga addict
CISPES activist
squash champion
vegan
acupuncturist
health nut
bookstore browser
organic farm worker
cat rescuer
Saturday morning lounger
rainy day sleeper

and this is now. And now I am mom.
And it's good.

CARDSTOCK: Kraft paper by Michelle Coleman (ScrapArtist)

PATTERNED PAPER: Color Me Happy by Michelle Coleman (ScrapArtist)

RUB-ON: Round and Round by Rhonna Farrer (Two Peas in a Bucket)

TITLE LETTERS: Offset Alphabet by Kellie Mize (Designer Digitals)

FONT: Certified

Simple Structure This layout is slightly off center to add to the sense of whimsy. The colors are bright and playful, and the title lettering is partially "empty" to reinforce the theme of bubbles.

Simple Story This is the sort of thing that happens all the time. Luca or Julian become fixated on some particular toy. The obsession lasts for, oh, about 20 minutes. Since it happens so often with different toys, I decided it was the perfect subject to scrapbook.

Simple Technique Printing your text sideways is a great way to tell your story while still keeping a tight design. The circular sunburst element helps bridge the gap between the journaling and the title while adding a fun splash of color. Notice how the elements are gathered together to create a tight layout design with plenty of white space.

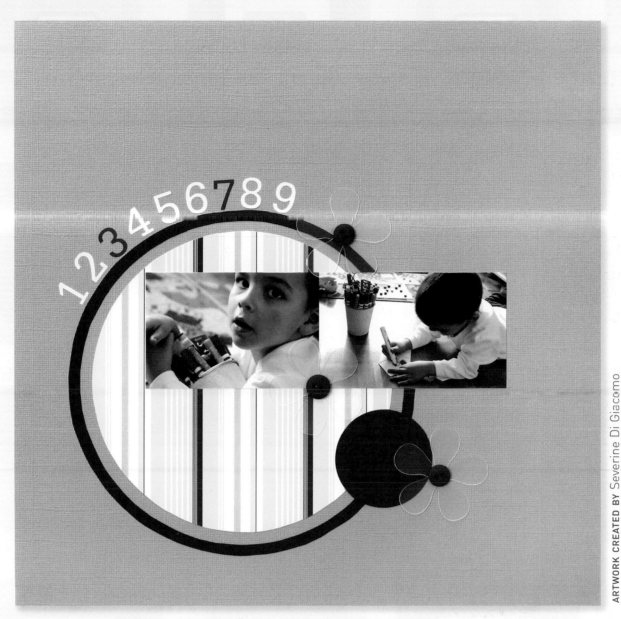

1 2 3 4 5 6 7 8 9

Journaling translation: In your very first "coin-coin" there is a heart, a little man who smiles, a star, a flower, the sun, the moon, and a little man who cries.

Simple Structure This delicate layout showcases two sweet photos of Severine's little artist. The circle draws your eye into the photo on the right. Soft clear flowers gently highlight the layout without overwhelming it. The small, dainty photos and the surrounding white space adds to the overall sense of light elegance on this page.

Simple Story Severine says, "I like to play with forms and colors. Nothing is better than to contrast lines against circles, soft colors against rich ones."

Simple Technique Create a small circle of text using image-editing software when you only have a few sentences you wish to share.

SUPPLIES

CARDSTOCK: Bazzill

PATTERNED PAPER: Me & My Big Ideas

NUMBER STICKERS: American Crafts

BUTTONS: American Crafts

FLOWERS: Maya Road

FONT: Arial

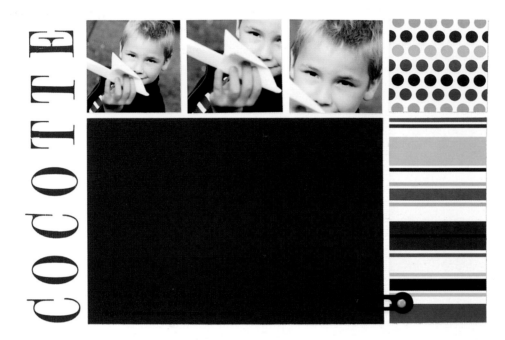

SUPPLIES

CARDSTOCK: Bazzill

PATTERNED PAPER:
American Crafts

RUB-ON LETTERS: American Crafts

MINI BRAD: American Crafts

PHOTO TURN: 7gypsies

FONT: Tw Cen MT

Simple Structure This layout proves that you don't need to have a wildly different structure to create a stunning layout. Severine used a strip of playful patterned paper and left a relatively large swatch of red cardstock empty. A few small, well-placed embellishments complete the layout.

Simple Story Severine says, "Because I didn't have many photos of this moment, I simply cropped my main photo in three different ways to create a geometric design and played with squares, rectangles and patterned papers to achieve the final result."

Simple Idea Journal on just a portion of a block of cardstock, and leave the remainder as white space.

Journaling translation: You are the king of paper shapes, airplanes and boats are no longer difficult for you and your bedroom is regularly invaded by your creations.

Simple Structure While not technically "white space," the expanse of red patterned paper is a simple way to create a beautiful, eye-catching layout without a lot of fuss. By placing her main elements tucked away at the bottom of the layout, Celeste created a mood of playful secrecy.

Simple Story Celeste says, "I don't have a lot of decent childhood photos of memories I would like to scrap. Sometimes you can get away with taking a picture of an object you have on hand to represent something in your story. Here, I thought the reader would be intrigued by the title and wonder why the picture was there—my attempt to draw the viewer in."

Simple Idea Using a photo of an object is a great way to relive a memory, when you don't have any photos from the time you'd like to scrap. Is there an object in your possession that tells a story?

SUPPLIES

CARDSTOCK: Bazzill

PATTERNED PAPER: Urban Lily

BRADS: American Crafts

FONT: District Thin, Little Days

ADHESIVE: Tombow

childhood confession

I bet your thinking what does scotch tape have to do with a childhood confession? Well, it was an important tool in one of my evil childhood escapades. Each Christmas, my sister and I would go into the attic and drag out the bags of toys from Santa. We would carefully slice the tape away from a present with a pocket knife and unwrap the gift with care and precision. Then we would cleverly scotch tape over every piece of tape we broke; rewrapping the gifts so that on cursory inspection my parents would never notice our crime. We pretended to believe in Santa for years and knew every year almost every gift we were getting. Rotten, huh?

ARTWORK CREATED BY Celeste Smith

SUPPLIES

CARDSTOCK: Bazzill, Prism

PATTERNED PAPER: Hambly

RUB-ONS: Die Cuts With A View, Hambly

LETTER STICKERS: KI Memories

BRADS: American Crafts, SEI

CHIPBOARD: Maya Road

PAINT: Delta

3D GLAZE: Ranger

FONT: Tw Cen MT

Simple Structure By using black cardstock as the background for this stunning layout, Nichole allowed her photos to pop off the page. And mimicking the look of flowers for frames? Genius!

Simple Story Nichole says, "As much as I want to scrapbook every photo in my collection, I simply can't. By creating a layout with a few of my favorite pictures, I could scrapbook those that weren't even related to each other and may have gotten lost in the shuffle."

Simple Technique Nichole put a unique spin on stitch rub-ons by using them as stems for her flowers. Can you think of an unusual way to use your more basic supplies?

ARTWORK CREATED BY Nicole Pereira

bookbag

A simple bookbag, a backpack actually, who knew what it would mean to you? You were so excited when I asked you to pick it out. You insisted on black with your name embroidered on it. You kept asking when it was coming. When it finally arrived, you took it right out of the packaging and immediately tried it on. Your first bookbag, just weeks until your first day of school, and me in tears in awe of how big you have become.

ARTWORK CREATED BY Celeste Smith

Simple Structure In this layout, Celeste used two patterned papers from the same line. The bold, geometric patterns create dimension when layered over the white space in the background.

Simple Story Celeste says, "When Adam put his backpack on for the first time, it really hit me that he was going to be heading off to kindergarten in a few short weeks. I knew I had to capture the moment so I ran for my camera, and wrote my journaling shortly after."

Simple Technique To achieve the look of white text on a dark background, you can use a word-processing program to "fill" your background with a dark color and convert the text color to white.

SUPPLIES

CARDSTOCK: Bazzill, Prism

PATTERNED PAPER:
American Crafts

LETTER STICKERS:
American Crafts

CHIPBOARD ARROW: KI Memories

FONT: Century Gothic

SOURCE GUIDE

THE FOLLOWING COMPANIES
MANUFACTURE PRODUCTS
FEATURED IN THIS BOOK. PLEASE
CHECK YOUR LOCAL RETAILERS TO
FIND THESE MATERIALS, OR GO TO
A COMPANY'S WEB SITE FOR THE
LATEST PRODUCT INFORMATION. IN
ADDITION, WE HAVE MADE EVERY
ATTEMPT TO PROPERLY CREDIT
THE ITEMS MENTIONED IN THIS
BOOK. WE APOLOGIZE TO ANY
COMPANY THAT WE HAVE LISTED
INCORRECTLY, AND WE WOULD
APPRECIATE HEARING FROM YOU.

3L Corporation
(800) 828-3130
www.scrapbook-adhesives.com

3M
(800) 364-3577
www.3m.com

7gypsies
(877) 749-7797
www.sevengypsies.com

American Crafts
(801) 226-0747
www.americancrafts.com

Arctic Frog
(479) 636-3764
www.arcticfrog.com

Atomic Cupcake
www.atomiccupcake.com

Autumn Leaves
(800) 588-6707
www.autumnleaves.com

BasicGrey
(801) 544-1116
www.basicgrey.com

Bazzill Basics Paper
(480) 558-8557
www.bazzillbasics.com

Chatterbox, Inc.
(888) 416-6260
www.chatterboxinc.com

CherryArte
(212) 465-3495
www.cherryarte.com

Club Scrap, Inc.
(888) 634-9100
www.clubscrap.com

Crate Paper
(801) 798-8996
www.cratepaper.com

Creative Imaginations
(800) 942-6487
www.cigift.com

Creative Memories
(800) 468-9335
www.creativememories.com

Creative Xpress
(800) 563-8679
www.creativexpress.com

Daisy D's Paper Company
(888) 601-8955
www.daisydspaper.com

Delta Technical Coatings, Inc.
(800) 423-4135
www.deltacrafts.com

Designer Digitals
www.designerdigitals.com

Designfruit
www.designfruit.com

Design by Dani
www.designbydani.com/store

Die Cuts With A View
(801) 224-6766
www.diecutswithaview.com

Digi Chick, The
www.thedigichick.com

DMC Corp.
(973) 589-0606
www.dmc-usa.com

Doodlebug Design Inc.
(877) 800-9190
www.doodlebug.ws

Duck Products - see Henkel Consumer
Adhesives, Inc.

Dymo
(800) 426-7827
www.dymo.com

Everlasting Keepsakes
(816) 896-7037
www.everlastinkeepsakes.com

Fancy Pants Designs, LLC
(801) 779-3212
www.fancypantsdesigns.com

Hambly Studios
(800) 451-3999
www.hamblystudios.com

Heidi Grace Designs, Inc.
(866) 348-5661
www.heidigrace.com

Heidi Swapp/Advantus Corporation
(904) 482-0092
www.heidiswapp.com

Henkel Consumer Adhesives, Inc.
(800) 321-0253
www.ducktapeproducts.com

Herma GmbH
www.herma.com

Imagination Project, Inc.
(888) 477-6532
www.imaginationproject.com

Imaginisce
(801) 908-8111
www.imaginisce.com

Jen Wilson Designs
www.jenwilsondesigns.com

Jo-Ann Stores
www.joann.com

Junkitz
(732) 792-1108
www.junkitz.com

K&Company
(888) 244 2083
www.kandcompany.com

KI Memories
(972) 243-5595
www.kimemories.com

Kuretake
www.kuretake.co.jp/uk

Luxe Designs
(972) 573-2120
www.luxedesigns.com

Making Memories
(801) 294-0430
www.makingmemories.com

me & my BiG ideas
(949) 583-2065
www.meandmybigideas.com

Memories Complete, LLC
(866) 966-6365
www.memoriescomplete.com

MOD — My Own Design
(303) 641-8680
www.mod-myowndesign.com

My Digital Muse
www.mydigitalmuse.com

My Mind's Eye, Inc.
(800) 665-5116
www.mymindseye.com

Pixel Decor
www.pixeldecor.com

Pocket Pearls
www.pocket-pearls.com

Prima Marketing, Inc.
(909) 627-5532
www.primamarketinginc.com

Prism Papers
(866) 902-1002
www.prismpapers.com

Queen & Co.
(858) 613-7858
www.queenandcompany.com

QuicKutz, Inc.
(888) 702-1146
www.quickutz.com

Ranger Industries, Inc.
(800) 244-2211
www.rangerink.com

Sakura Hobby Craft
(310) 212-7878
www.sakuracraft.com

Sassafras Lass
(801) 269-1331
www.sassafraslass.com

Scenic Route Paper Co.
(801) 225-5754
www.scenicroutepaper.com

ScrapArtist
(734) 717-7775
www.scrapartist.com

Scrapbook Graphics
www.scrapbookgraphics.com

Scrapworks, LLC / As You Wish Products, LLC
(801) 363-1010
www.scrapworks.com

SEI, Inc.
(800) 333-3279
www.shopsei.com

Shabby Shoppe, The
www.theshabbyshoppe.com

Stampin' Up!
(800) 782-6787
www.stampinup.com

Stemma/Masterpiece Studios
www.masterpiecestudios.com

Sweet Shoppe Designs
www.sweetshoppedesigns.com

Tombow
(800) 835-3232
www.tombowusa.com

Tsukineko, Inc.
(800) 769-6633
www.tsukineko.com

Two Peas in a Bucket
(888) 896-7327
www.twopeasinabucket.com

Urban Lily
www.urbanlily.com

We R Memory Keepers, Inc.
(801) 539-5000
www.weronthenet.com

Xyron
(800) 793-3523
www.xyron.com

Zig - see Kuretake

sugar high*

Sunday

What can I say? I'm ashamed to say this is the first layout I've ever done about you. And you've been in my life for... let's see. 15 years. Yep, you've lived through graduate school in Vermont, a tiny apartment in Hell's Kitchen, countless trips to Long Island to visit my mom. You were through at least five teary breakups. You've patiently and kindly put up with the innumerable stray animals that I brought home through the years. And then, of course, I had my boys, and you were relegated to a second priority in my life. And for that I am sorry You are very special to me. You don't mind when Julian hugs you too tightly. You patiently remind me when I forget to fill your bowl with fresh water (and yes, I will try not to forget the ice cubes.) You are a pretty cat mellow and calm, you love to sleep on my neck at night. I just wanted to say thanks, Sunday, for being such a wonderful companion to me, and to my family, for all these years. (journaling written 08/26/07)

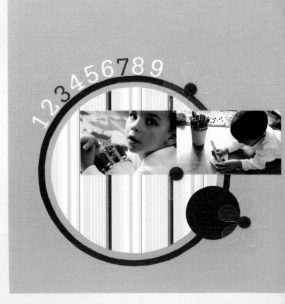

artist biographies

HILLARY HEIDELBERG

I've been scrapbooking for a little over five years and it has truly become my passion. I love creating sharp, clean designs that capture the everyday moments in my life. I live right in the heart of Manhattan with my two young boys, Luca and Julian, and my wonderful husband, Michael. In addition to working on design teams for **Die Cuts With A View** and **We R Memory Keepers**, I teach online classes at **http://www.nycscraps.com**. My hobbies include reading fiction, running and playing with my boys.

SEVERINE DI GIACOMO

I live in a small village in the French-speaking part of Switzerland. I work part-time as a teacher and am the mother of two boys ages 8 and 5. I discovered scrapbooking in 2003 thanks to the Internet. At that time scrapbooking was almost unknown in Europe. Today I am on the International Design Team for American Crafts and the first Swiss Design Team for Scrapdeco. My style of scrapbooking is simple—sometimes graphic and sometimes classic. This style allows me to focus on my photos and the story I want to tell. I have been published in *Creating Keepsakes*, *Memory Makers*, *Simple Scrapbooks*, *Scrapbook Answers* and in the books *Freestyle* (Autumn Leaves) and *Simply Graphic* (Memory Makers).

TRACEY ODACHOWSKI

At home, I'm the wife of Chris, the mama to Gabe and Emily, and the back door opener to Zuzu. At work, I'm a registered nurse. Late at night, when I'm taking a break from those roles, I'm a scrapbooker. This crazy passion of mine began when I had a night off from work and stepped into a Creative Memories party. I haven't looked back. After years of trying to find the style that was most comfortable, I finally realized I kept reverting back to cleaner lines with just enough embellishments to enhance the theme. I like to keep the focus on my photos, and my simpler pages do that effectively. A 2007 Creating Keepsakes Hall of Fame inductee, my work can be seen in *Creating Keepsakes*, *Memory Makers*, *Scrapbooks, etc.* and *Simple Scrapbooks*.

NICHOLE PEREIRA

I am a 27-year-old Californian and work as a children's and teen librarian. Although I've been scrapbooking for about eight years, only in the last few years have I truly found my "groove." I usually scrap in an 8.5" x 11" format, both portrait and landscape—I guess you could say I am "square-impaired." I love to use simple supplies and embellishments; some of my favorites include cardstock, brads, letter stickers and my craft knife. I was on the Scrapbook Answers design team and co-authored a book with Design Originals titled *Scrapbooks on the Go*.

AMANDA PROBST

I'm a homeschooling mom of three fabulous boys. In my "spare" time, I happen to scrapbook. I love to bring photos, stories and lines together and revel in the challenge of doing so in a way that conveys true feeling... whatever that feeling may be. In doing this, I lean toward the clean and simple, although I love to experiment with new techniques and ideas when I can find the time. My natural tendency, however, is to follow the "less is more" philosophy, to ensure the emphasis is on my story, not my embellishments.

CELESTE SMITH

I live in Connecticut with Terry, my wonderful husband of ten years and our two cute boys, Adam and Sam. They are my primary scrapping subjects and my sometimes unwilling models. Scrapbooking is my creative outlet. As a full-time competitive analyst at a large insurance company, my days are filled with details and numbers. My evenings are filled with patterns, color and design. A real stress reliever! I have only been scrapbooking for two and a half years but my style has been consistently clean and graphic with a bit of funkiness thrown in for good measure. I have been published in *Scrapbook Trends*, *Creating Keepsakes*, *Memory Makers*, *Simple Scrapbooks* and *Scrapbooks, etc.*, as well as numerous books and online publications. Recently, I was honored to be in the Top 15 in the Making Memories Idol.

index

Discover more inspiration and ideas with these Memory Makers Books!

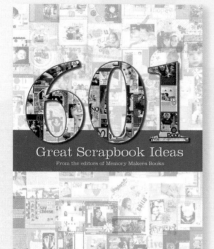

601 Great Scrapbook Ideas
Brimming with inspiration and ideas, you'll discover one amazing page after another in this big book of layouts.

ISBN-13: 978-1-59963-017-5
ISBN-10: 1-59963-017-6

paperback
272 pages
Z1640

Ask the Masters! Making the Most of Your Scrapbook Supplies
Innovative and inspiring ideas from the Memory Makers Masters for using that growing stash of scrapbook supplies and tools.

ISBN-13: 978-1-59963-012-0
ISBN-10: 1-59963-012-5

paperback
128 pages
Z1040

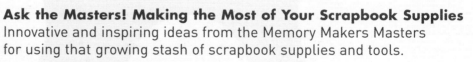

Quick & Easy Scrapbook Styles
Learn the tricks and techniques for making quick scrapbook pages in a range of popular styles including graphic, sassy, urban, fun + funky and romantic.

ISBN-13: 978-1892127-98-3
ISBN-10: 1-892127-98-9

paperback
128 pages
Z0523